GOD'S LOVE LETTER
REFLECTIONS ON 1 JOHN

WILL VAUS

GOD'S LOVE LETTER:
REFLECTIONS ON I JOHN

Copyright © 2014 Will Vaus

Barnabas Books
a Division of Winged Lion Press
Hamden, CT

All rights reserved. Except in the case of quotations embodied in critical articles or reviews, no part of this book may be reproduced or transmitted in any form or by any means, electronic or mechanical, including photocopying, recording, or by any information storage or retrieval system, without written permission of the publisher.
For information, contact Winged Lion Press www.WingedLionPress.com

Winged Lion Press titles may be purchased for business or promotional use or special sales.

Unless otherwise noted Scripture references are taken from the HOLY BIBLE, NEW INTERNATIONAL VERSION ®. Copyright © 1973, 1978, 1984 International Bible Society.
Used by permission of Zondervan. All rights reserved.

10-9-8-7-6-5-4-3-2-1

BARNABAS BOOKS

ISBN 13   978-1-935688-06-8

Dedication

For Kevin, Mario & Tom
Three mentors
who have shown me
the love of God

Contents

Introduction	1
John, Jesus & Our Purpose in Life	3
Walking in the Light	8
Dealing with Sin	15
The Marks of a Christian	23
Where the True Light Shines	30
Something Not to Love	37
Warning about the Anti-Christ	43
Staying on Course	50
Living in God's Family	54
Who Is A Real Christian?	61
Love One Another	68
Confidence before God	75
Test the Spirits	82
God's Love & Ours	89
Blessed Assurance	95
Faith & Its Effects	102
Four Witnesses	109
The Benefits of Being a Christian	117
Conclusion	125
Endnotes	127
For Further Reading	131

Introduction

Dr. Leo Buscaglia, who for many years taught a class at the University of Southern California entitled "Love 1A" once said, "Love is life. And if you miss love, you miss life."

I believe that is true. If this was the last book that I ever wrote, the most important thing I could write about is love. That consideration is, in fact, what determined my writing … not that I expect to die tomorrow. It is just that I realized I have never written a book about the most important subject in the world.

So as I sat down to think about love, as a Christian, I naturally wondered: What book of the Bible talks most about love?

Do you know the answer?

The word "love" appears some 551 times in the Bible. 319 of those times are in the Old Testament. 144 of those are in the Psalms; that is almost one mention of love per psalm. Therefore, if we were looking for the book of the Bible that talks most about love it would be the Psalms.

The New Testament mentions love 232 times. 103 of those are in the letters of Paul. Of course, 1 Corinthians 13 is known as the Love Chapter in the Bible. However, if we were looking for one book of the New Testament that talks more about love than any other, it would be the First Letter of John. 1 John uses the word love 35 times. That is quite a lot for five chapters.

The Bible is sometimes called God's love letter to humanity. In some sense, I imagine that is true. However, I think if we were looking for one particular letter of love in the Bible, it would have to be 1 John.

Now, I have to state a caveat right at the beginning. 1 John is not like most other letters in the New Testament. It is not addressed to a specific group of people. It does not begin with "Dear So and So" and it does not end with "Yours sincerely, John." What is called the first letter of John is really more like a sermon or a meditation. David Jackman describes 1 John as being like a spiral staircase. He writes,

> As you climb the central staircase in a large palace or a stately home, you see the same objects or paintings from a different angle, often with a new appreciation of their beauty. It is rather like that with the great

truths John is concerned to state and revisit in the letter. The view gets more wonderful as you climb and the heavenly light shines more and more clearly until you reach the top.[1]

Who created this wonderful spiral staircase and when was it created? This is one of only two letters in the New Testament (the other one being Hebrews) that does not provide the author's name. However, the opening verses of 1 John seem to suggest that the author heard, saw, and even touched Jesus of Nazareth. Furthermore, there are many similarities in language and topics between 1 John and the Gospel of John. Finally, it was the unanimous opinion of the Early Church that 1 John was written by John, the disciple of Jesus. The most important attestation to this came from Irenaeus who was a disciple of Polycarp who in turn was a disciple of John.

However, modern scholars have, for a number of reasons, suggested that 1 John was written by a disciple of John the Evangelist, rather than by John himself. It seems likely that a group of disciples gathered around John the Evangelist, possibly in Ephesus, and that one or more of these disciples was responsible for collecting and editing what John wrote about Jesus in his Gospel. Thus, we have two endings to the Gospel of John: one in chapter 20 and another, added by one of John's disciples, consisting of the whole of chapter 21. It seems likely that one or more of these disciples of John also collected the meditations we have in 1 John.

In either case, whether 1 John was written by John the Evangelist or by one or more of his disciples, scholars are agreed that 1 John was most likely written toward the very end of the first century, around AD 90 or perhaps as late as 100, probably from Ephesus in Asia Minor. The conservative, evangelical scholar, Donald Guthrie, once wrote about 1 John,

> In one sense the authorship is not the most important issue, for the exegesis of the letter is not greatly affected by our conclusions regarding authorship.[2]

With all of this background in mind, let us dive into reading this letter about love for ourselves and see what we can learn from it about our greatest need and, in fact, the greatest need of our world. Even though 1 John is a brief letter, it is packed with deep, spiritual truth. Therefore, I would encourage you to read one chapter of this book per week, or at most, one chapter per day. Then, take time to ponder and let the significance of "God's Love Letter" sink deep into your heart....

JOHN, JESUS & OUR PURPOSE IN LIFE

> That which was from the beginning, which we have heard, which we have seen with our eyes, which we have looked at and our hands have touched—this we proclaim concerning the Word of life. The life appeared; we have seen it and testify to it, and we proclaim to you the eternal life, which was with the Father and has appeared to us. We proclaim to you what we have seen and heard, so that you also may have fellowship with us. And our fellowship is with the Father and with his Son, Jesus Christ. We write this to make our joy complete. (1 John 1:1-4)

In these opening four verses of 1 John the author, whom I will call John, for lack of any other name, tells us three important things: about his purpose, about himself, and about Jesus. Let us look first at what John tells us about his purpose in writing....

First, John tells us it is his desire for his readers to have fellowship with them. As I have already suggested, the "we" and the "us" in the opening of this letter probably refers to the group of disciples gathered around John the Evangelist in Ephesus. John's desire is that his readers would have fellowship with them, and he states that their fellowship is with the Father and his Son, Jesus Christ.

Fellowship, koinonia, was a very important word designating a vital experience in the life of the early church. As it was used in classical Greek, koinonia was a common way of expressing the intimate bond of the marriage relationship. Here and throughout the New Testament, koinonia describes the Christian's personal relationship with God through his Son, Jesus Christ, and the Christian's relationship with other Christians.

At its most basic level, koinonia means: "sharing in common". What we share in common as Christians is a personal relationship with the Father and the Son; the church is a family.

Thus, John's purpose in writing this letter, or this sermon, this meditation, is to draw his readers closer to each other and closer to God. That ought to be our purpose in life as well. Do our words and our actions draw people closer to each other and closer to God?

Second, John says his purpose is to bring his readers joy. "We write this to make our joy complete."

Joy is at the heart of Christianity. Paul tells us joy is an essential part of the fruit of the Spirit (Galatians 5). If the effect of our words and our actions is to depress others, to bring them down, then we must ask if our words and our actions are truly Christian. Our purpose should be to lift people up into the joy of a relationship with God through his Son Jesus Christ.

Third, John says it is his aim to set Jesus Christ before his readers. "We proclaim to you what we have seen and heard…"

What do others see and hear in us? Jesus Christ, or something less? We will never be completely like Jesus in this life, but it should be our goal to become more like him, by the power of the Holy Spirit, so that our very lives will proclaim him.

What is your purpose in life? What is mine? Is it to draw people closer to each other and closer to God? Is it to bring joy to others, to lift them up rather than tearing them down? Is our purpose to proclaim Christ in all we say and do?

Victor Frankl, who lived through the Holocaust, loved to quote Friedrich Nietzsche who said, "He who has a 'why' to live can bear almost any 'how'." In other words, having a purpose in life can pull you through almost any circumstance without imploding. I believe the highest and the most stable purpose in life is, as the Westminster Catechism states: "to enjoy God and glorify him forever". That is the greatest thing we can do in life. However, we will never reach the end of that goal. There is always more to discover about God, enjoy about God, and glorify about God.

In addition to telling us three things about his purpose in writing, John tells us four important things about himself.

First, John says that he has heard that which was from the beginning: "That which was from the beginning, which we have heard…"

The prophets in the Hebrew Scriptures were always ones who had a "word from the Lord". (Jeremiah 37:17) I think this is one reason why people come to church, or to religious institutions of any kind. They do not come to hear another person's opinions or guesses about God. They come hoping to hear a word from the Lord. A wonderful way to approach church is to ask the Lord to speak to you and through you during your time in worship, and then actively look for the ways God will do just that. It was said of John Brown of Haddington that when he preached he would often pause as if listening for another voice. William Barclay says, "The true teacher is the man who has a message from Jesus Christ because he has heard his voice." Whoever the author of 1 John was, he made this very claim, that he had heard the voice of God.

Reflections on 1 John

Second, John says that he has seen that which was from the beginning. "That which was from the beginning, which we have heard, *which we have seen with our eyes...*"

The story is told about the great Scottish preacher Alexander Whyte that someone once said to him, "You preached today as if you had come straight from the presence."

Whyte's response was to say, "Perhaps I did."

We do not see Jesus Christ in the body today as the first disciples did. However, we can see Jesus through the eyes of faith. Paul says, "We walk by faith, not by sight." (2 Corinthians 5:7)

Third, John tells us he has gazed upon that which was from the beginning. What is the difference between seeing and gazing? In Greek, the word that is used for seeing is "horan" and simply means to see with our physical eyes. On the other hand, the word that is used for "gazed" or "looked at" is "theasthai" and that word means to gaze at someone or something until one grasps the significance of that person or thing.

1 John echoes the prologue of John's Gospel where the Evangelist says about Jesus, "We beheld his glory." The verb that is used in that case is also "theasthai". The author of 1 John, like the author of the Gospel, has thought long and hard about who Jesus was and is, trying to understand something of the mystery of the incarnation: God taking on our human flesh in Jesus of Nazareth.

Fourth, John says that he has touched that which was from the beginning.

I think the author of 1 John is doing two things here. He is recalling how, in the Gospel of John, the disciple whom Jesus loved reclined on Jesus' breast or bosom at the Last Supper.

Second, the author of 1 John is responding throughout this letter or meditation to a group of people later called the Docetists. The name "Docetist" comes from the Greek word "dokeo" which means: "to seem". The Docetists maintained that Jesus only seemed to have a human body. The Docetists believed that if Jesus was really divine then he would not dirty himself by having a human body.

John's response to this is strong and categorical. He insists throughout his letter that Jesus did indeed have a human body and that Jesus' disciples touched this human body; Jesus was not a spirit simply "seeming" to appear in a body; he really inhabited one.

Drawing these four things together that the author of 1 John tells us about himself, we can see that the author had a real and true experience of the word of life that appeared in Jesus of Nazareth.

William Hendricks writes in his book, *Exit Interviews*,

> There is a splendid moment in the movie Jurassic Park, when world-

> class paleontologist Allen Grant, who has devoted his life to the study of dinosaurs, suddenly comes face-to-face with real, live prehistoric creatures. He falls to the ground, dumbstruck. The reason is obvious. It is one thing to piece together an informed but nonetheless imperfect image of dinosaurs by picking through fossils and bones. But to encounter an actual dinosaur—well, there can be no comparison.
>
> For many people, spirituality amounts to picking through the artifacts of faith that survive from long ago and far away. In that bygone era, humans saw God, heard His voice, and experienced his awesome, at times terrible, power. But that was then. Today, those kinds of gripping encounters with God—with a God who wasn't an illusion, but Someone who was real, Someone you could see, and touch, and feel—well, there could be no comparison.[3]

We may not be able to see Jesus now with our physical eyes, or to touch him with our hands, but we can nonetheless have a true experience of Jesus through the power of the Holy Spirit living in us.

This leads to John's final point in his mini-prologue to this letter or meditation: he tells us something important about Jesus.

John tells us that Jesus was from the beginning. Again, our author is echoing the prologue to the Gospel: "In the beginning was the Word…" The author of 1 John emphasizes the divinity of Jesus.

Yet, in the same breath he emphasizes Jesus' humanity as well. Jesus had a human body that could be seen and touched and his human voice could be heard.

John tells us that by God taking on human flesh in Jesus of Nazareth, he has thereby brought to us and to the world, the word of life that can impart to us the life of the ages.

Again, 1 John is echoing the opening of the Gospel of John which talks so much about the Word, the Logos, the Greek idea of the reasoning power behind the universe. Both the Gospel and 1 John identify this Logos with Jesus.

This is the only place where the exact phrase "the word of life" appears in the Bible. However, Paul talks about "a word of life" in Philippians 2:16. Beginning with Philippians 2:14 we read…

> Do everything without complaining or arguing, so that you may become blameless and pure, children of God without fault in a crooked and depraved generation, in which you shine like stars in the universe as you hold out a word of life—in order that I may boast on the day of Christ that I did not run or labor for nothing.

Paul and the author of 1 John are both saying the same thing: we have a word to offer to people that can bring them life. That being the case, how can we hold back on offering that word in the midst of a dying world?

Matt Woodley writes…

> Psychologist Madeline Levine has been counseling teenagers for over 25 years, but recently Levine has begun to see a new breed of unhappy teenagers—smart, successful, and privileged kids who feel utterly lost and empty. For Levine, one client in particular typified this kind of unhappy teenager. Late on a Friday afternoon—the last appointment of her week—Levine saw a 15-year-old girl who was "bright, personable, highly pressured by her adoring, but frequently preoccupied … parents." The girl was also "very angry."
>
> Levine quickly recognized the girl's "cutter disguise"—a long-sleeve t-shirt pulled halfway over her hand, with an opening torn in the cuff for her thumb. Such t-shirts are used to hide self-mutilating behaviors: cutting with sharp instruments, piercing with safety pins, or burning with matches. When the young girl pulled back her sleeve, Levine was startled to find that the girl had used a razor to carve the following word onto her forearm—"EMPTY."

Levine commented:

> I tried to imagine how intensely unhappy my young patient must have felt to cut her distress into her flesh…. The most common thing I hear in my office from the kids is, "I'm fake." The surface of [their family life] always looks good…. The lawns are always perfectly manicured, the houses always look beautiful. But when you get to what's going on beneath these kids' T-shirts, there's not much happening inside.[4]

Into such an "empty" world where nothing seems "real", even into our own empty worlds of unreality, God speaks his word of life in Jesus: a life that offers us fullness instead of emptiness, joy instead of despair, life instead of death, real love instead of the apathy of "fake" relationships. The word of life is something, some One really, whom we are called to embrace for ourselves, and carry to others in our world who very much need "the life of the ages".

Walking in the Light

I find it fascinating that every time there is a tragedy of some kind in our world, people are soon gathering at churches or other locations and lighting candles in memory of loved ones who have died. It seems our instinctive response as human beings confronted with so much darkness is to try to let a little bit of light shine through the gloom.

Light and darkness is the subject of 1 John 1:5-7....

> This is the message we have heard from him and declare to you: God is light; in him there is no darkness at all. If we claim to have fellowship with him yet walk in the darkness, we lie and do not live by the truth. But if we walk in the light, as he is in the light, we have fellowship with one another, and the blood of Jesus, his Son, purifies us from all sin.

John tells us he has a message that he and his community have heard from Christ and that they have to pass on. This message includes at least three important things we need to know about light. First, he tells us that God is light. There is no darkness at all in God.

Notice that John says God IS light. God is not simply like light; he *is* light. Light is so much associated with God's character that the two are inseparable.

Think back to the beginning of the Bible: "God said, 'Let there be light' and there was light." It was the first thing God created. All creation owes its existence and its sustenance to light.

At the Exodus, when Yahweh led his people Israel out of slavery in Egypt, he guided them using a glory cloud by day and a pillar of fire by night—the "shekinah" glory of God.

Jesus said, "I am the light of the world. Whoever follows me will never walk in darkness, but will have the light of life." (John 8:12)

Then at the very end of the Bible, when we are introduced to the City of God, the New Jerusalem, we read, "And the city has no need of sun or moon to shine on it, for the glory of God is its light, and its lamp is the Lamb. The nations will walk by its light, and the kings of the earth will bring their glory into it. Its gates will never be shut by day—and there will be no night there." (Revelation 21:23-25)

God is light. What does this statement tell us about God?

It tells us that God is full of splendor and glory. What is more glorious than the light of the rising sun piercing the darkness of the night, scattering the shadows?

It tells us that God is revealing. C. S. Lewis once said, "I believe in Christianity as I believe that the Sun has risen, not only because I see it, but because by it I see everything else."[5]

In the same way, I can say, "I believe in God as I believe in the sun, not because I see him, but because by him I see everything else." God is the great revealer. His light shows us life as it really is.

This statement, "God is light," also suggests something of the purity and holiness of God. There is nothing of darkness in him in which evil can hide.

It also tells us of the guidance of God. Light shows the way. The road that is well lit is the easiest one to follow. To say that God is light is to say that he offers his direction to our steps. He is a lamp to our feet and a light to our path. (Psalm 119:105)

In addition to telling us that God is light, *John very emphatically tells us that there is no darkness in God at all.* As we shall see as we move through our study of 1 John, the author is almost obsessed with these dramatic contrasts: light versus darkness, good versus evil, love versus hate, righteousness versus sin, obedience versus disobedience, faith versus unbelief, love of the Father versus love of the world, life versus death.

As William Barclay points out, darkness stands for the very opposite of the Christian life, for the Christ-less life, the life that is hostile to the light, ignorant, chaotic, immoral, unfruitful, and loveless. Thankfully, though, we do not have to remain in the darkness. Rather, we can step into the light of Christ by the power of the Holy Spirit.

During a trip to England some time ago, I rented a car. On the last two days of my trip, I had some free time so I decided to drive from London down to visit Canterbury Cathedral in the south. Then my plan was to drive back from there to catch my plane out of London on Monday.

Now, I had driven in England before this particular trip, and so I already had experience driving on the left-hand side of the road. What I did not factor into the equation was that I would be driving on roads I had never been on before, and due to my schedule and the time of year, I would be doing some of that driving in the dark.

As the sun went down during my drive from London to Canterbury, I suddenly realized what a ridiculous plan I had made. I began to wonder: "What if I cannot find the right roads to take in the dark? What will I do if I cannot find my hotel?"

Well, I did find my way and I had a wonderful time in Canterbury, but then I faced the same problem driving back to London the next night. All I can tell you is that I prayed a lot during the drive down to Canterbury and during the drive back to London. I did make it through without any mishaps, but it would have been a lot easier to do the drive both ways in the light of day.

Now imagine if I had tried to drive both directions without any light at all. That drive would have gone from difficult to impossible. At least I had the help of headlights on my rental car, lighted signs, and lighted roads.

I believe what the author of 1 John is suggesting to us is that trying to navigate our way through life without God is kind of like my trying to drive from London to Canterbury and back without any physical light at all. We need the light of God to guide us through life.

The second thing John tells us is that if we claim fellowship with God, but walk in darkness, we lie and do not live by the truth.

John here may have been responding to an early form of what was later called Gnosticism. Remember, in the last chapter I talked about the Docetists who believed that Jesus only appeared or seemed to have a human body. The Docetist was a type of Gnostic. The Gnostics believed that this world was created by some lesser deity, and therefore, this world and the body in particular, are evil, but spirit is good. The whole goal of religion, then, according to the Gnostic, is to free the spirit from the body. This is achieved through secret "gnosis" or knowledge.

It seems that the Gnostics had two approaches to dealing with the body. Some thought the best approach was to deny all the desires of the body. These Gnostics focused on fasting and denied that institutions like marriage were any good at all. Other Gnostics, apparently, taught that it does not matter what one does with the body since it is evil anyway.

It is an early form of this latter type of Gnosticism to which John may have been responding. In effect he says: "You say that you are walking in the light of a special, secret knowledge of God and his ways, yet your evil deeds deny this, because you act like it does not matter what we do with our bodies. But it does matter!"

In response to this Gnostic way of thinking, John asserts two important points. *First, if we claim to have fellowship with God, who is light, then we must walk in the light.*

William Barclay explains,

> This does not mean that a man must be perfect before he can have fellowship with God; if that were the case, all of us would be shut out. But it does mean that he will spend his whole life in the awareness of his obligations, in the effort to fulfill them and in penitence when he fails. It will mean that he will never think that sin does not matter; it will mean that the nearer he comes to God, the more terrible sin will be to him.

Reflections on I John

Second, John asserts that the early Gnostics have the wrong idea of truth. If we claim some special enlightenment, but still walk in darkness, then we are not *doing* the truth, we are not living it out, and that is all-important.

We read something very much like this in John 3:21, "But whoever lives by the truth comes into the light, so that it may be seen plainly that what he has done has been done through God."

This means that for Christians, truth is not simply some intellectual exercise of the mind. If we believe certain things with our minds, it should also change the way we live. Truth involves thinking *and* acting. If we spend all our time merely studying the Bible and discussing what it says, but it does not affect how we live, then we have missed what Christianity is all about.

The story is told of a desert nomad who woke up in the middle of the night and was extremely hungry. He kept a bowl of dates beside his bed for just such occasions, but he had to light a candle in order to see them. The nomad took a bite from one of the dates and found a worm in it, so he threw the rotten date outside of his tent. He tried another date, found another worm, and threw that date away as well. Finally, the nomad concluded that if things continued on like this he would not have any dates left to eat and he was very hungry. Therefore, the nomad blew out the candle and continued eating the dates.

There are many who prefer darkness and denial to the light of reality. However, that is not the way God wants us to live. He does not want us to go on eating rotten dates.

So what is the answer? We need to step out of the darkness and into the light.

Martin Luther King, Jr. once said, "Darkness cannot drive out darkness: only light can do that. Hate cannot drive out hate: only love can do that."

This leads to the third point that John makes: that if we walk in the light, we have two things. *The first thing we have is fellowship with other Christians.* In darkness, we walk alone, but in the light, we walk with a great company of saints.

Once again, I love what William Barclay says about this. He writes,

> Truth is the creator of fellowship. If men are really walking in the light, they have fellowship one with another. No belief can be fully Christian if it separates a man from his fellow-men. No Church can be exclusive and still be the Church of Christ. That which destroys fellowship cannot be true.

This reveals that the darkness John was especially concerned about in verse six, was the darkness of believing that we can have fellowship with God without at the same time maintaining fellowship with other followers of Christ. This was part of the error of the early Gnostics. They were dividing their followers from the rest of the Church by claiming that they alone had a superior knowledge.

The more that we walk in the light of Christ, the more we will recognize our need to lay down our weapons of hatred, condemnation, and destruction, so that we may walk hand in hand with our brothers and sisters and thus bring to realization the kingdom of God.

David Jackman has written,

> Where Christians are at variance, or separate from one another, it is always true that someone is already walking out of fellowship with Christ. This does not mean that we shall all agree about everything, but that is not the essence of fellowship anyway. It is about loving one another and valuing one another, so that we can agree to differ without severing the ties that bind us to one another as sons and daughters of the light.

I have had times in my life where it was very hard for me to see, let alone accept, this truth. I remember so well when I first went to Princeton Theological Seminary in New Jersey. I was just twenty-two years old, but I knew my Bible and, looking back, I probably thought I had all the answers, or most of them anyway. I had such a hard time that first year at Princeton. I was learning so many new things, hearing so many things I disagreed with, meeting people who were very different from me.

I remember sitting down with Sam Moffett, Professor of Missions, who I knew to be a good Christian. We had lunch together and I laid out all my concerns before him. He listened to all that I had to say very quietly and then he spoke these few words: "Being with people you agree with all the time isn't missionary."

That was it? I thought there had to be something more. However, I thought about those eleven words for a long time, and eventually I chose to stay at Princeton Seminary. Now, looking back many years later, I am so glad that I did.

If we are walking in the light of Jesus' love, we will walk hand in hand with all those who claim him as Lord and Master, even if we do not agree about everything all the time.

The final thing John tells us in our passage for today is that: *if we walk in the light, we have cleansing by the blood of Christ.*

The more we come into the light, the more we become aware of our own dirtiness, but that also creates an opportunity to have our dirt washed away.

C. S. Lewis once wrote these words to a former student whom he had the opportunity to lead to faith in Jesus Christ....

> I know all about the despair of overcoming chronic temptations. It is

not serious provided self-offended petulance, annoyance at breaking records, impatience etc doesn't get the upper hand. No amount of falls will really undo us if we keep on picking ourselves up each time. We shall of course be v. muddy and tattered children by the time we reach home. But the bathrooms are all ready, the towels put out, & the clean clothes are in the airing cupboard. The only fatal thing is to lose one's temper and give it up. It is when we notice the dirt that God is most present to us: it is the v. sign of His presence.[6]

It is so easy to read John's statement as simply one of general Christian truth: "The blood of Jesus cleanses us from all sin." However, as William Barclay points out, it ought to mean so much more than that. It ought to be a present reality for us. "All the time, day by day, constantly and consistently, the blood of Jesus Christ ought to be carrying out a cleansing process in the life of the individual Christian."

Is Jesus doing that work in your life by the power of the Holy Spirit? He is doing that work and he will continue to do it, if you ask him.

The Greek word that is used here for cleansing is a beautiful one; it is "katharizein" from which we get our English word "catharsis".

Catharsis has been defined as "a sudden emotional breakdown or climax that constitutes overwhelming feelings of great pity, sorrow, laughter, or any extreme change in emotion that results in renewal, restoration, and revitalization."

The Greeks held this as the goal of their great dramatic productions. It is true that this happens for many people, even to this day, in watching a great film, or play, or when listening to a grand piece of music or viewing a fantastic work of art.

We see catharsis taking place when Nathan confronts David about his sin of stealing Uriah's wife, Bathsheba, and killing Uriah. Rather than confront David directly, Nathan tells him the following story in 2 Samuel 12....

> There were two men in a certain town, one rich and the other poor. The rich man had a very large number of sheep and cattle, but the poor man had nothing except one little ewe lamb he had bought. He raised it, and it grew up with him and his children. It shared his food, drank from his cup and even slept in his arms. It was like a daughter to him.
>
> Now a traveler came to the rich man, but the rich man refrained from taking one of his own sheep or cattle to prepare a meal for the traveler who had come to him. Instead, he took the ewe lamb that belonged to the poor man and prepared it for the one who had come to him.

David burned with anger against the man and said to Nathan, "As surely as the Lord lives, the man who did this must die! He must pay for that lamb four times over, because he did such a thing and had no pity."

Then Nathan said to David, "You are the man!"

At this, David broke down and confessed his sin.

Sometimes, like David, it is easier for us to see our own sin reflected in a story. However, the catharsis is not complete, until we come to Jesus and ask him to cleanse us. God does not want us to remain in our guilt. He wants us to experience the fullness of his love and forgiveness.

David Slagle has written,

> Recently my 21-month-old, who had just learned to say, "Daddy," had been struggling with asthma and an ear infection for two weeks. He coughed and sneezed continually, and his nose ran like a faucet. Each night when I came home, he ran to meet me at the door, smiling, coughing, nose running, yelling, "Daddy! Daddy!"
>
> I was not repulsed by his runny nose or close range sneezes in the least (he "slimed" every shirt I own!). I love him deeply and enjoy his love for me.
>
> I'm reminded that though I am sick with sin, God loves me deeply and desires that I run to him as a son crying, "Abba, Father."

So that we may be encouraged to move from the darkness into the light, let us always remember what the Apostle Paul once wrote,

> For I am convinced that neither death nor life, neither angels nor demons, neither the present nor the future, nor any powers, neither height nor depth, nor anything else in all creation, will be able to separate us from the love of God that is in Christ Jesus our Lord. (Romans 8:38-39)

Dealing with Sin

After I moved out from my parents' home at age eighteen, my brother Roger was my first roommate. My parents were very kind and gave us a sofa bed of theirs to put in the living room of our apartment. I well remember transporting that sofa bed from my parents' home to our apartment in an open, flatbed, pick-up truck. We had to travel on an interstate highway to get from the point of pick up to drop off, and at one point along the highway, one of the back cushions to the sofa bed flew out of the bed of the truck. My brother Roger quickly pulled over to the side of the highway and parked. We both got out of the vehicle and ran back to the side of the road beside the spot where the sofa cushion was lying in the middle of the road. There was just one problem. This was in California and there were cars constantly whizzing past us at 55 miles per hour or faster. The good news was that all of the cars were going around the sofa cushion … that is … until we got back to the place where we could run out and retrieve the cushion. Just at that moment in time, a truck came along and plowed right over the cushion, sending up a cloud of feathers.

Roger and I were rather down in the mouth about this. There was no way that we were going to be able to hide from our parents what had happened to the sofa bed cushion. Our parents would soon be coming over to see our new apartment and celebrate with us. It would be obvious when they walked into our living room that the sofa was missing a cushion, and it was all because of our carelessness in not securing the cushion for transport in the first place.

We all have a similar, though bigger problem in life. The Bible calls that problem "sin". We have all thought, said or done things that are wrong, and not just by accident, but many times on purpose. Furthermore, there is no way to hide our sin from our all-knowing heavenly Father. The question is, "What are we going to do about dealing with our sin problem?"

In 1 John 1:8-10, John shows us two dead ends when it comes to dealing with our sin problem, and one way through….

> If we claim to be without sin, we deceive ourselves and the truth is not in us. If we confess our sins, he is faithful and just and will forgive us our sins and purify us from all unrighteousness. If we claim we have not sinned, we make him out to be a liar and his word has no place in our lives.

The first dead end that John talks about is *the denial of the sinful nature.*

"If we claim to be without sin, we deceive ourselves and the truth is not in us." Here we must go back to basics and ask: What is sin?

The word means simply "to miss the mark" or "to fall short of a target".

Think of shooting arrows. We pull back the arrow on the string and let it fly. Then imagine that the arrow, not only misses the bull's eye, but falls short of the target altogether. Perhaps we try again. We move closer to the target and shoot, but then the arrow misses the target once more. Then imagine realizing that no matter how many times you move closer to the target and shoot your arrow again, you miss, because the target is an infinite distance away.

God created us perfect, but now, no matter how hard we try in our own power, we cannot hit the target. We fall short. We sin.

William Barclay says, "To fail to be as good a father, mother, wife, husband, son, daughter, workman, person as we might be is to sin; and that includes us all."

It seems that John may have been combating the error of some people to whom he was writing who denied that they even had a sinful nature. Many people down through history have denied that they have a sinful nature. Some people today say that our human problem is not sin, but lack of education. They suggest if we are educated properly then our problems will gradually disappear. Education is a wonderful thing. I am glad that I have had all the educational opportunities I have had. I want as many people in the world as possible to have as much education as possible. However, education alone will not solve our moral problems. Education alone does not provide a relationship with God. We live in perhaps one of the most well educated ages of all time, yet humanity's problems have not gone away.

For the past two thousand years, the Church has taught that God created human beings perfect, but that humanity has fallen from that original goodness and now we all have a sinful nature. Education has not and cannot solve our sin problem. Paul says in Romans 5:12 that "sin entered the world through one man, and death through sin, and in this way death came to all men, because all sinned." John says that if we deny this, then we are deceiving ourselves and the truth is not in us.

Brian Coffey writes,

> My mother's grandfather was a coalminer in the hills of eastern Kentucky. She called him Grampa Joe. By all accounts he lived hard, worked hard, and drank hard most of his life. When he was sober, he was the loving and beloved patriarch of the clan; he told wonderful stories, and the grandkids loved to sit on his lap. But when Grampa Joe was drinking, he would disappear for weeks at a time, choosing whiskey and brothels over wife and family.

Reflections on I John

> Late in his life, Grampa Joe contracted liver disease from the alcohol and black-lung disease from the coalmines. He was hospitalized, waiting for death to come. My mother, who was 19 years old at the time and a brand-new Christian, went to visit her beloved Grampa Joe. She cared about him and wanted him to know that God loved him. She wanted him to have the chance to respond to the forgiveness available in Christ. So she sat by his bed and gently outlined the message of the gospel to Grampa Joe.
>
> After listening politely to her presentation, Grampa Joe looked up and said, "I don't believe I've ever sinned."
>
> She was shocked, because the whole family knew about his lifestyle. She said, "But Grampa, we've all done bad things. Can't you think of just one thing you've done that was wrong?"
>
> He pretended to think for a minute, and then said, "I take it back, I take it back. I have sinned—once. I voted Republican one time."[7]

I am sorry to say it, but it must be said: Grampa Joe was headed toward a dead end.

The second dead end John talks about is *the denial of sinful actions*.

Some people may not deny that human beings have a sin nature in some general sense, yet they still fail to see how they, specifically, have committed any sins. This attitude may not be as uncommon as you think.

When I was at Princeton Seminary every Master of Divinity student had to spend some time in field education. We would be assigned to some church or ministry, have a supervisor, and the supervisor would report on our ministry experience, and we would get credit that would count toward our degree.

My best friend in seminary, Richard Burnett, who was from the South, was assigned for a time to a Presbyterian church in the Philadelphia area. On Sunday evenings, when we returned to the seminary from our field assignments, Richard and I would often get hoagies from our favorite Princeton restaurant, Hoagie Haven, and we would bring our sandwiches back to his room or mine, and we would chat together over our informal dinner.

I will never forget the Sunday evening when Richard said to me, "You won't believe what I heard in my adult Sunday School class today."

I said, "Try me."

Richard proceeded to tell me, "There was this man in my class, an elder in the church. He came up to me after the Sunday school lesson and he said, 'Richard, I have just one problem with what you said this morning. I don't think I have ever sinned.'"

Richard was so taken aback by this that he paused for a moment and thought about the situation. Then he thought of a counter question. He said to this elder in the church, "We are having Communion today. If you have not sinned, why do you reckon Jesus died on the cross?"

The elder responded, "For the sins of humanity."

Richard asked, "Do you reckon you are part of humanity?"

I do not remember how that conversation ended, but it is a startling example of the fact that there are people, even people in leadership in Christian congregations, who do not believe they have ever sinned, though they would not deny that other human beings have sinned.

However, this is not the only way that sinful actions are often denied, even by Christians. Some Christians, while admitting that they have sinned in the past, deny that they sin any more.

Even as great a Christian leader as John Wesley believed that Christians could attain some form of perfection in this life. Now, I do not claim to be any expert on Wesley's theology. However, the older I get the more unrealistic such claims as these, from Wesley and others, appear to me. For example, Wesley made this statement at the age of 82:

> I am never tired in my work. From the beginning of the day or the week or the year to the end I do not know what weariness means. I am never weary of writing or preaching or travelling; but am just as fresh at the end as at the beginning. Thus it is with me today, and I take no thought for tomorrow.

It is futile to argue with someone's experience, but I have often wondered if Wesley's wife would have had the same perspective on Christian perfection, especially her husband's own "perfection", as Wesley himself did.

I believe that 1 John 1:8-10 and passages like Romans 7 argue against any doctrine of Christian perfection. Paul, speaking as a mature Christian says in Romans 7,

> I do not understand what I do. For what I want to do I do not do, but what I hate I do. And if I do what I do not want to do, I agree that the law is good. As it is, it is no longer I myself who do it, but it is sin living in me. I know that nothing good lives in me, that is, in my sinful nature. For I have the desire to do what is good, but I cannot carry it out. For what I do is not the good I want to do; no, the evil I do not want to do—this I keep on doing. Now if I do what I do not want to do, it is no longer I who do it, but it is sin living in me that does it.
>
> So I find this law at work: When I want to do good, evil is right there with me. For in my inner being I delight in God's law; but I see another law at work in the members of my body, waging war against the law of my mind and making me a prisoner of the law of sin at work within my members. What a wretched man I am! Who will rescue me from this body of death?

John says that if we claim we have not sinned, then we make God out to be a liar and God's Word then has no place in our hearts.

I actually find such passages of Scripture as 1 John 1:8-10 and Romans 7 encouraging. Verses such as these remind me, that if I still find sin in my life, after being a Christian for almost forty years, I need not be despondent. The bottom line is this: Christians continue to sin in this life, right up to death's door. Therefore, if you are still a sinner, and if I am still a sinner (and I am), then we are in good company.

Martin Luther talked about being at the same time a sinner *and* justified (declared righteous in God's sight through faith in Jesus Christ). That is where we are as Christians in this life: "Simul just et peccator," at the same time justified and sinners.

I like Charles Haddon Spurgeon's response to the idea of Christian perfectionism. The story is told about Pastor Spurgeon being confronted by a man who claimed to be without sin. Intrigued by the man's claims, Spurgeon invited the man into his own home for dinner. After listening attentively to this man's claims of perfection for quite some time over their shared meal, Spurgeon suddenly threw a glass of water in the man's face. Naturally, the man was rather upset and expressed his anger toward Spurgeon rather forcefully. To this Spurgeon replied, "Ah, you see the old man within you is not dead, he had simply fainted and could be revived with a glass of water!"

Sometimes it does not take much to reveal our sin nature.

Thus, John shows us two dead ends when it comes to dealing with sin. One is to deny the sinful nature altogether, the other is to deny specific sinful actions in some way or another. However, what is the solution, what is the way through? Are we then simply to sit down and be content with our sinful condition?

No. Thankfully, John tells us the proper way to deal with sin. The way through that John points out is *confession*.

What does it mean *to confess?* The Greek word that is translated as *confess* means "to say the same word". In other words, to confess means to say the same word that God says. When God says that we are his adopted children through Christ, and we agree with that and say that it is true, then we are making a confession. When God says that we are sinners, and when he convicts us of specific sins, by the power of his Spirit working through Scripture, and we agree with God's statement, then we are confessing sin.

John says that if we do our part and confess our sins, then God will do his part and forgive us. Specifically, John says that God is faithful and just in order to forgive us.

Now, we can perhaps understand what John means when he says that God is faithful. In this context, God is faithful to his promise to forgive. He has promised that when we confess our sins, he will forgive us. He is faithful to that promise every time we confess. However, how is God just? After all, if God was really just he would condemn us for our sins because that is what our sins deserve, is it not?

That is true. However, justice in this context refers to a different aspect in God's nature and plan. Tom Wright explains that in the death of Jesus God has shown himself to be just, to be in the right. Through the death of Jesus, God is putting the whole world to rights, and us with it. We will talk more about this in the next chapter.

However, for now, we need to make sure we see one more thing that John tells us. That one more thing is that when we confess our sins, God is not only faithful and just to forgive us, to let go of our sins, so to speak, but God promises to purify us of all unrighteousness. There is a two-fold action, and it takes place every time we confess sins. First, God forgive us of our sins, he lets them go, because we have agreed with him about our sin, we have come clean about it, and because Jesus has died on the cross for our sins. As if that was not good enough, God does one thing more: he cleanses us completely of our sin, and in fact, he gives us the righteousness of his Son Jesus Christ.

Paul puts it this way in 2 Corinthians 5:21, "God made him who knew no sin to be sin for us, so that in him we might become the righteousness of God." That is what God did for us on the cross in his Son Jesus Christ. Now, because that is true, every time we confess our sins, every time we agree with God and say, "Yes, I am a sinner, I have done this, or said this, or thought this, and it was wrong," then God forgives us and he purifies us, he gives us the righteousness of Christ. It is like waking up one morning to find out that some rich uncle has not only paid all of our debts, but he has put a million dollars in our bank account to boot.

One interesting thing to note in this regard is that when it comes to the importance and the value of confession, theology and psychology are in agreement. Matt Woodley writes,

> Two diverse sources—ancient Christian monasticism and modern psychology—agree on at least one thing: keeping dark secrets can destroy us, and confessing them can set us free. The fifth century Christian spiritual leader John Cassian claimed that "as soon as a wicked thought has been revealed [to God and at least one other Christian] it loses its power." The demonic stronghold of sin is "drawn out as it were into the light from its dark and [deep] cave by the power of the confession.... For [Satan's] harmful counsels hold sway in us as they lie concealed in our heart."

Nearly 1,500 years later, a contemporary textbook on psychology reached a similar conclusion (although note Cassian's emphasis on sin and demonic strongholds). The book *Coping with Stress* claims that "people who tend to keep secrets have more physical and mental complaints, on average, than people who do not ... [including] greater anxiety, depression, and bodily symptoms, such as back pain and headaches." Like Cassian, this book also argues that finding healthy places to share our secrets leads to freedom: "The initial embarrassment of confessing is frequently outweighed by the relief that comes with the verbalization of the darker, secretive aspects of the self."[8]

Even though theology and psychology agree on the importance and value of confession, it is also interesting to note how theological and psychological communities of study diverge in some ways when it comes to the actual practice of confession and the solution to the underlying problems that we confess. In her book, *Hope Has Its Reasons*, Becky Pippert writes about attending two very different events on the same day. One was a graduate-level psychology class at Harvard University and the other was a Christian Bible study adjacent to Harvard. Pippert offers the following observations in her book on how the two groups addressed (or failed to address) their faults, problems, and sins:

> First, the students [in the graduate-level psychology class] were extraordinarily open and candid about their problems. It wasn't uncommon to hear them say, "I'm angry," "I'm afraid," "I'm jealous".... Their admission of their problems was the opposite of denial. Second, their openness about their problems was matched only by their uncertainty about where to find resources to overcome them. Having confessed, for example, their inability to forgive someone who had hurt them, [they had no idea how to] resolve the problem by forgiving and being kind and generous instead of petty and vindictive.
>
> One day after the class, I dropped in on a Bible study group in Cambridge. [The contrast] was striking. No one spoke openly about his or her problems. There was a lot of talk about God's answers and promises, but very little about the participants and the problems they faced. The closest thing to an admission [of sin or a personal problem] was a reference to someone who was "struggling and needs prayer."
>
> The first group [the psychology class] seemed to have all the problems and no answers; the second group [the Bible study] had all the answers and no problems.[9]

The fact of the matter is that as Christians we have both problems and answers. We need to find places where and people with whom we can be totally honest about our problems and our sins, but we also need places and people in our lives that can remind us of the answer in Jesus Christ, the one who became sin for us, so that in him we might become the righteousness of God.

You may be wondering what happened with the sofa bed I mentioned at the beginning of this message.

What happened was that we were honest with my parents about what happened to the cushion, and they supplied a solution to the problem: some pillows judiciously placed to *replace* the missing cushion.

Our God says that if we are honest with him about our sins, he will not only forgive us, but replace the missing cushion, torn up by our sinful choices, with something even better: the righteousness of his Son Jesus. Let us thank him for that indescribable gift ... .

The Marks of a Christian

In the last chapter, I talked a good bit about God's forgiveness. One possible response to that forgiveness is to say something like: "Well, if God is going to forgive us, no matter what we do, then we might as well go on sinning, right?"

In one sense, it is good that people say this. The only way people can say this is if they have begun to grasp something of the enormity, the grandeur, of God's love and mercy.

However, do you remember my illustration from the last chapter about the sofa bed that my parents gave to my brother and me when we moved into an apartment together? We foolishly allowed one of the cushions from the sofa bed to fly out of our truck, and another truck ran over it on the freeway. Thankfully, my parents graciously replaced that cushion with some throw pillows.

Now, here is my point. To say that: "we might as well go on sinning however we want since God is going to forgive us anyway" would be kind of like my brother and I saying, "let's throw the whole sofa bed out on to the freeway since Mom and Dad will give us a new one". To say such things, just does not make sense. The whole goal of forgiveness is restoration and re-creation, not further destruction.

In the second chapter of First John, the author continues to maintain the delicate balance between reminding us of God's forgiveness for our past and present mistakes, and encouraging us to step into a new life of re-creation. As John maintains this delicate balance, he also points out three marks of the Christian. See if you can recognize those marks as we read from First John 2:1-6....

> My dear children, I write this to you so that you will not sin. But if anybody does sin, we have one who speaks to the Father in our defense—Jesus Christ, the Righteous One. He is the atoning sacrifice for our sins, and not only for ours but also for the sins of the whole world.
>
> We know that we have come to know him if we obey his commands. The man who says, "I know him," but does not do what he commands is a liar, and the truth is not in him. But if anyone obeys his word, God's

love is truly made complete in him. This is how we know we are in him: Whoever claims to live in him must walk as Jesus did.

What John says here suggests that there are at least three marks of a Christian. John is a realist. He recognizes Christians are not perfect, just forgiven. Thus, he also recognizes that Christians are not complete. In this life, we are always in process. Therefore, as we look at the marks of the Christian life we must always remember that these marks are signs that are *beginning* to appear in the life of every Christian. These marks are not fully developed, and will not be evident in their full glory, until the day we stand before Jesus and he makes us whole in his presence.

When I was in college I participated in a community drama production directed by a professional actor from Hollywood. The man's name was Eric Christmas. All of us in the production were very excited to be working under a real, Hollywood actor. However, as rehearsals for the play wore on, we discovered that our real, Hollywood actor/director also had a real temper. Whenever we failed to live up to his expectations, he could really let loose with some angry comments.

Finally, Mr. Christmas realized, perhaps because someone had tipped him off, that his angry outbursts were having a detrimental effect upon the cast. Thus, he gathered us all together one evening and apologized for his behavior. Furthermore, he quoted Michelangelo who, in the year 1562, at the age of 87, wrote these two simple words on a sketch he was doing: "Ancora imparo." Translated, that means: "I am still learning."

I believe every human being needs this sort of perspective on life. I believe every Christian ought to have this perspective: I am still learning.

When I first came under care of a presbytery in preparation for ministry I had to give a statement of my faith in front of a room full of ministers. I began by saying, "I am still *becoming* a Christian, a Christ-in person."

I still think that is true. I am still *becoming* a Christian. The process is not yet complete in me, or in you.

With these thoughts in mind, let us look at the marks of the Christian life that John presents to us here. First, a Christian is one who is beginning *to know who Christ is.*

John tells us a few important things here that we can know about Christ. First off, *Christ is the one who speaks to the Father in our defense.* The Greek word used here is παρακλητον. This word is used in John's Gospel in reference to the Holy Spirit. It means, literally, "one who is called to come alongside". Jesus is our advocate before the Father, our helper, and our counselor.

Therefore, what John is saying, is that *if* we sin (it really should be *when* we sin; John knows we are going to sin but he does not want to encourage it) when we sin we have an advocate before the Father; we have one who speaks in our defense. That advocate is Jesus. Jesus does not condemn us. He does not despise us. He does not reject us, even in our sin. No, he opens the way for us to the Father; he heals and restores. That is who Jesus is: healer, restorer, helper, advocate, counselor, and comforter. Jesus is the one who comes alongside of us, even in our sin; he puts his arm around each one of us and says: "Here, let me help you."

Think about what Jesus' name means. His name does not mean "Yahweh hates us" or "Yahweh condemns us" or "Yahweh rejects us". Jesus' name means "Yahweh saves". Our God is always the One who saves, restores and heals.

Christ means Messiah, anointed one. Among the Jews, three people, especially, received anointing: prophets, priests and kings. Jesus is our great prophet speaking to our needs. He is our high priest, interceding for us and sacrificing himself for us. Jesus is our benevolent king: always loving, always caring, always guiding, and always providing for us.

Jesus is also "the Righteous One". Back when I was growing up, in the days of the Jesus movement, in the days of the hippies, people used to say: "That's righteous!" or: "He's righteous!" or: "She's righteous." To call someone or something "righteous" was a complement like saying it, or she, or he, was right on! I think we need to recover that sense of "righteous".

These days we tend to think of "righteousness" only in terms of someone who is self-righteous, sanctimonious, or holier-than-thou. Jesus was none of these things. With whom did he spend his time? Jesus was famous for hanging out with sinners, with prostitutes, with tax collectors, with all the people that the religious leaders did not want to have anything to do with. In his righteousness, Jesus did not separate himself from people in need. Rather, he identified with them. He loved them. Furthermore, Jesus still loves people who recognize their need and he wants to show them the right way of living. I believe that is what we should think of when we think of the righteousness of Jesus. He was right on! If we want to know what righteousness is, then we look at Jesus. He is the definition of it. His picture should be next to the word in the dictionary.

Do we know this Jesus of whom John speaks? Are we, at least, beginning to know him?

As William Barclay explains, in the ancient world, there were three different pathways delineated for knowing God. The great Greek philosophers, like Plato and Socrates, thought they could arrive at knowledge of God by reason alone. The later Greeks, around the time of the events recorded in the New Testament, believed they could come to knowledge of God through emotional experience. We talked about this earlier in terms of the use of Greek drama to produce a cathartic experience, an experience of cleansing and healing, but primarily emotional. Then there were the Jews, who believed that human beings receive knowledge of God not primarily through reason, nor through emotion, but rather through revelation. In a sense, knowing God really involves all three of these things. Ultimately, we cannot know God unless he reveals himself to us. Christianity claims that God has revealed himself supremely in Jesus of Nazareth, and because God has revealed himself in Jesus we can come to know him in a way that involves our reasoning powers, our emotions, and our will—more on the last point in a few moments.

However, again, the question is: do we know Jesus, or do we just know about him? Is our knowledge personal? Is it relational, or is it just a thing of the mind?

George Mallory was an English mountaineer who took part in the first three British expeditions to Mount Everest in the early 1920s. Mallory and his climbing partner both disappeared somewhere high on the northeast ridge during their attempt to make the first ascent of the world's highest mountain.

Before his disappearance, someone asked Mallory, "Why do you want to climb Mount Everest?"

His famous answer was, "Because it is there."

On another occasion Mallory expanded his answer. He said,

> If you cannot understand that there is something in man which responds to the challenge of this mountain and goes out to meet it, that the struggle is the struggle of life itself upward and forever upward, then you won't see why we go. What we get from this adventure is just sheer joy. And joy is, after all, the end of life.

In a letter to his wife, Ruth, Mallory revealed even more about what drove him to climb the mountain. "Dearest," he wrote, "You must know that the spur to do my best is you and you again…. I want more than anything to prove worthy of you."

However, though George Mallory became famous for his achievements, his son John had a different perspective. Proud of his father but sad too, John Mallory later wrote, "I would so much rather have known my father than to have grown up in the shadow of a legend, a hero, as some people perceive him to be."[10]

I wonder, do we know Jesus merely as some distant legend, or do we know him personally and intimately? Jesus longs for us to know him, and to know his heavenly Father, not as some distant, famous person, but as a close and loving parent. A Christian is one who is at least beginning to know Christ in this way.

Second, a Christian is one who is beginning *to trust what Christ has done*.

The main thing John tells us that Christ has done for us is that "He is the atoning sacrifice for our sins, and not only for ours but also for the sins of the whole world."

The goal of most religions is for human beings to know God, to have fellowship with God. However, there is something in the way; it blocks our access to God. The Bible calls that impediment "sin". In ancient times, every Jew learned from an early age that fellowship with God was restored through sacrifice.

The word that is used here, that is translated as "atoning sacrifice", is ιλασμος. The word can mean "to pacify the wrath of God". It can also refer to God's forgiveness. Thirdly, the word may refer to some deed that is performed by which guilt, the taint of sin, is removed. C. H. Dodd said that we need to be "disinfected" from our sins so that we can enter into the presence of our holy God. John is probably bringing all these meanings together when he says that Jesus is the atoning sacrifice for our sins.

Paul uses a form of this same word in Romans 3:25 when he says that God presented Jesus as a sacrifice of atonement. The word as Paul uses it is the same word that is used in the Greek translation of the Hebrew Scriptures for "mercy seat". The mercy seat was the place on top of the Ark of the Covenant, between the golden carved wings of the cherubim, where the High Priest sprinkled the blood of the sacrifice on the Day of Atonement. Paul is telling us, and I think John is saying the same thing, that Jesus is our mercy seat. Jesus is the place where we find atonement, at-one-ment with God. Jesus is the place where our sins are covered.

William Barclay says, "Jesus is the person through whom guilt for past sin and defilement from present sin are removed. The great basic truth behind this word is that it is through Jesus Christ that man's fellowship with God is first restored and then maintained."

John was probably writing, at least in part, to Jewish Christians, who were tempted to think that Jesus, as Israel's Messiah, was the sacrifice for their sins and theirs alone. John quickly corrects any such notion. He says, "No, Jesus is not simply the sacrifice for our sins, but also for the sins of the whole world, not just for Jews, but for everyone." Everyone is included.

When I was in high school, I taught a fifth-grade Sunday school class. I remember a particular Sunday when we were talking about the death of Jesus and how, at the moment of Jesus' death on the cross, the curtain in the Temple that divided the Holy Place from the Holy of Holies was torn in two from top to bottom.

Immediately, one of my fifth grade boys shot up his hand. He said, "Do you know why the curtain was torn from top to bottom?"

I said, "No, why?"

This ten-year-old boy replied, "Because God did it. Only God could have reached high enough to tear the curtain in the Temple from top to bottom."

I said, "You are absolutely right!"

My ten-year-old Sunday school student understood the truth that Bible commentator David Jackman expresses so well:

> The thick veil, or curtain, which separated the worshipper from the holiest place of all, which only the High Priest was allowed to enter once a year on the Day of Atonement, was torn in two, from top to bottom, by the hand of God, not man. It is as though God was saying to the whole world of sinners, "You may come in now."

John says that the Christian is one who is at least beginning to trust in what Jesus has done to open the way for human beings to enter into God's presence.

Finally, John tells us, a Christian is one who is beginning to *walk as Christ walked*.

How do we know that we know Jesus? John says that we can know that we know Jesus if we obey his commands. Knowledge of Jesus involves our minds, it involves our emotions, our hearts, but it also involves our will, it involves actions. Anyone who says that he or she knows Jesus, but who does not do what Jesus commands, is, according to John, a liar. However, if we do obey Jesus then God's love is made complete in us. This is how we know we are *in* Jesus (those two words, *in Jesus*, provide a wonderful way of describing an intimate relationship with Christ): we can know we are in Jesus if we will begin to walk as Jesus walked.

How did Jesus walk? What are his commands?

According to Matthew 22:36-40, a Pharisee once asked Jesus,

> "Teacher, which is the greatest commandment in the Law?"

> Jesus replied: "'Love the Lord your God with all your heart and with all your soul and with all your mind.' This is the first and greatest commandment. And the second is like it: 'Love your neighbor as yourself.' All the Law and the Prophets hang on these two commandments."

That is how Jesus walked. That is how he lived his life: Loving God the Father with all his heart, soul and mind, and loving his neighbor as himself. That is how Jesus lived and that is how he wants us to live. Love is the sum and substance of his commands.

Author and speaker Brennan Manning has an amazing story about how he got the name "Brennan". While growing up, Manning's best friend was another young man named Ray. The two of them did everything together. They bought a car together as teenagers, they double-dated together, and they went to school together. The two young men even enlisted in the Army together;

they went to boot camp together and fought on the frontlines together. One night while sitting in a foxhole, Manning was reminiscing about the old days in Brooklyn while Ray listened and ate a chocolate bar. Suddenly a live grenade came into the foxhole. Ray looked at Manning, smiled, dropped his chocolate bar and threw himself on the live grenade. The grenade exploded, killing Ray, but Manning lived.

When Manning became a priest, his teachers instructed him to take on the name of a saint. He thought of his friend, Ray Brennan. Therefore, Manning took on the name "Brennan".

Years later, Manning went to visit Ray's mother in Brooklyn. They sat up late one night having tea when Manning asked her, "Do you think Ray loved me?"

Mrs. Brennan got up off the couch, shook her finger in front of Manning's face and shouted, "What more could he have done for you?"

Manning said that at that moment he experienced an epiphany. He imagined himself standing before the cross of Jesus wondering, "Does God really love me?" and Jesus' mother Mary pointing to her son, saying, "What more could he have done for you?"

On the cross, Jesus did all he could do to show his love for us. Still, we often wonder, "Does God really love me? Am I important to God? Does God care about me?" All we have to do is look to the cross to see God's answer, God's great "Yes, I love you!"

Our supernatural response to that love, should be to take Christ's name for our own, to call ourselves "Christians", little copies of Christ, "Christ-in" persons, and to live out the same kind of love he has shown to us.[11]

Do you see the marks of a Christian in your life? Are you at least beginning to know God as your loving heavenly Father through Christ? Are you beginning to trust in the love that Jesus has shown to you on the cross? Are you beginning to walk in love as Jesus walked? Jesus can make all of this possible, if you just ask him to help you. He is the great "paraclete" who longs to come alongside of you, put his arm around you, comfort, encourage, counsel, and lift you up.

Where the True Light Shines

Over the years that I have lived in Virginia, I have found that the hardest months for me to handle are January and February. This is the case because of the cold and the snow. However, even harder to handle are the dark, grey days, especially for a boy who grew up in Southern California.

Even for those who have not grown up in a sunny climate, overcast days are hard to handle. Why is that? That is the case because we all need sunshine. Sunlight gives us the Vitamin D we need that lifts our spirits.

What is true in the physical realm is also true in the spiritual. We need the light of God. The question is: where do we find it? John tells us where in 1 John 2:7-14….

> Dear friends, I am not writing you a new command but an old one, which you have had since the beginning. This old command is the message you have heard. Yet I am writing you a new command; its truth is seen in him and you, because the darkness is passing and the true light is already shining.
>
> Anyone who claims to be in the light but hates his brother is still in the darkness. Whoever loves his brother lives in the light, and there is nothing in him to make him stumble. But whoever hates his brother is in the darkness and walks around in the darkness; he does not know where he is going, because the darkness has blinded him.
>
> I write to you, dear children,
>
> because your sins have been forgiven on account of his name.
>
> I write to you, fathers,
>
> because you have known him who is from the beginning.
>
> I write to you, young men,
>
> because you have overcome the evil one.
>
> I write to you, dear children,
>
> because you have known the Father.
>
> I write to you, fathers,

because you have known him who is from the beginning.

I write to you, young men,

because you are strong,

and the word of God lives in you,

and you have overcome the evil one.

As I said at the beginning of this book, First John is like a spiral staircase. As the reader ascends the staircase, he or she revisits earlier themes, but the reader gets to see these themes from a new angle each time. Thus, John returns in chapter two to a theme he introduced in chapter one: light and darkness. In chapter two, John tells us about three places where the light of God shines.

First, the light shines in God's commands.

It is easy to think of God's commands as something handed down from on high by a cruel taskmaster. However, such is not the case. John introduces this next section of his letter by addressing his readers as "Beloved". That is who you are. That is who I am. That is who every person who has ever lived or ever will live *is*. We are all "beloved" in God's eyes.

Furthermore, in his love, God gives to us certain guidelines for living. Like a loving parent who guides a young child away from the things that will harm him or her and toward those things that will nurture his or her life. God's commands are not arbitrary, but rather God speaks his commands for our benefit.

John says that he is writing to remind his readers of a command that is both old and new. What command is John talking about?

If we go back to the Gospel of John, which our author almost certainly had in mind, we read about a new commandment that Jesus gave to his disciples. In John 13:34, Jesus said, "A new command I give you: Love one another. As I have loved you, so you must love one another."

This is really an old command in that God revealed it long ago in the Hebrew Scriptures. In Leviticus 19:18 we read: "Love your neighbor as yourself."

However, this commandment is new in the sense that it has reached a completely new standard in the life of Jesus. In the same way that Jesus loved us, God calls us to love one another, and Jesus loved us by laying down his life for us.

Love is also a completely new thing in Jesus, in terms of the extent to which it reaches. In Jesus, love reaches out to sinners. According to William Barclay, the orthodox Jewish rabbis used to say: "There is joy in heaven when one sinner is obliterated from the earth." By contrast, Jesus said: "There will be more rejoicing in heaven over one sinner who repents than over ninety-nine righteous persons who do not need to repent." (Luke 15:7) Jesus also said, "For God so loved the world that he gave his only begotten Son…" The world Jesus is talking about in John 3:16 is the world system that is set against God. God loves sinners so much that he gave us his Son.

The love of Jesus is also something new in terms of the length to which he goes to show his love to us. No human action, no lack of response on our part, did ever, or will ever, turn Jesus' love to hate. If he could pray from the cross, "Father, forgive them for they know not what they are doing," then obviously nothing will ever stop Jesus from loving you, loving me, loving everyone.

John's message is clear: Jesus takes loving to an entirely new level. What do I mean when I say Jesus takes loving to a new level? It is kind of like this….

Swimming is one thing when you watch me do it. I love swimming. I enjoy swimming in a pool or in the ocean. However, I have never been on a swim team. I do not know how to swim fast. I have never received advanced training in swimming.

It is another thing to watch Michael Phelps swim. He is the most decorated Olympian of all time, with twenty-two medals. Phelps has taken swimming to an entirely new level.

For another example, think of cooking. I loved the movie, *Julie and Julia*, all about the life and cooking of famous chef, Julia Child, and this woman, Julie, who tries to emulate her. I finished watching that movie and immediately wanted to cook some bœuf bourguignon for my family. Did I do it? No. Can I be a decent chef when I try? Yes. However, Julia Child took cooking to a new level. The whole world knows it.

Another example is singing. I think I am a good singer. I enjoy singing. I have even had some vocal training. However, Luciano Pavarotti was one of the greatest tenors this world has ever seen. He took singing to a completely new level.

It is the same thing with Jesus, only bigger. Michael Phelps certainly took swimming to a new level. Julia Child took cooking to a new level. Pavarotti took singing to a new level, but Jesus took loving to an entirely new level. Jesus shows us what real love is. He showed us on the cross.

God's light shines in his command to love, a command most perfectly fulfilled in Jesus.

The fact that God's light shines in his commands is inextricably tied to John's second point, that the light shines in *Christian love*.

God's light shines not only in God's command to love, fulfilled in Jesus' love, but his light shines in *our* love for one another, in and through us. How amazing is that?

However, we must note that John issues a warning here. The warning is this…. If we claim to be walking in God's light, yet we still hate our brothers and sisters, our fellow human beings, and especially our fellow Christians, then we are, actually, still living in darkness. In short: lack of love equals night.

On the other hand, if we love our brothers and sisters, our fellow Christians and fellow human beings in general, then we are walking in the light. Love equals daytime.

If we are walking in the light, then we will see where we are going and we will not stumble around. Literally, John says, "Offense in him is not". The word John uses that may be translated as "offense" or "cause of stumbling" is σκανδαλον. This is the Greek word from which we get our English word "scandal". In other words, if we are walking in the light by loving our brothers and sisters then there will be no scandal in us. That does not mean that others may not see scandal where there is none. Human beings have an amazing knack for stirring up scandal where it does not even exist. There is something about love that some people will always find scandalous. However, if we walk in love, then we can be sure that God sees no scandal in our lives, nothing that gives him offense.

Thus, we must make a decision, will we walk in love and sometimes have others wonder what we are up to, or even question our motives, or will we live bland, insipid, apathetic lives that never attempt the dangerous, scandalous experiment of love?

Once again, we see here how John thinks in terms of black and white. There is no grey area when it comes to love. Either we love our brothers and sisters, or we hate them.

Sheldon Vanauken, about whom I have written a biography, once said,

> The best argument for Christianity is Christians: their joy, their certainty, their completeness. But the strongest argument against Christianity is also Christians—when they are somber and joyless, when they are self-righteous and smug in complacent consecration, when they are narrow and repressive, then Christianity dies a thousand deaths.

Another way of putting this is to say that when we, as Christians, love others, then we are the greatest argument *for* Christianity, but when we fail to love, we are the greatest argument against the faith. The choice is ours: we can be excellent advertisements for Jesus or not. It all depends on love.

Thus, John has told us about two places where the light of God shines. The light shines in God's commands and it shines in Christian love. Thirdly, the light shines in words of encouragement.

John speaks words of encouragement here, seemingly, to three different groups in the church: children, young men, and fathers. If we take these terms to refer to spiritual maturity, rather than chronological age, then John is speaking to new Christians, those who are still young in the faith, and to those who are mature in the faith.

In addition to addressing three groups, John reminds these three groups of three gifts God has given them: forgiveness, knowledge, and strength. However, here there is an overlap. God gives knowledge of himself both to the children and to the fathers, to new Christians and to the mature. This suggests that, in actuality, all three gifts are for all three groups. Each of us still has a place within us where we are children, where we are young men and women, and where we are mature fathers and mothers in the faith. Those of us who are older can probably all identify with the feeling of youth we still sometimes carry in our hearts. Furthermore, the young among us can often say the wisest things, things that belong to maturity. "Out of the mouths of babes…."

Therefore, let us look more deeply at the three gifts that John reminds us of here, gifts that belong to all of us as followers of Christ….

First, there is *forgiveness*. "I write to you, dear children, because your sins have been forgiven on account of his name." Forgiveness of sins comes through the name of Jesus.

To the Jews, a name was not something which one simply called another person; a name represented the *character* of that person. The psalmist says, "Those who know your name put their trust in you." (Psalm 9:10) This does not mean that those who know the name of God, Yahweh, automatically trust in him. It means that those who have come to know God's character in an intimate, relational way will put their trust in him, for they know by experience that he is trustworthy.

Therefore, when John says that our "sins have been forgiven on account of his name", Jesus' name, he means that when we know the character of Jesus, when we have experienced him, then we are assured of forgiveness because forgiveness and love are essential aspects of the character of Jesus.

The second gift John reminds us about is *knowledge*. "I write to you, fathers, because you have known him who is from the beginning…. I write to you, dear children, because you have known the Father."

If John the disciple of Jesus was the author of this letter, then he may have been thinking about his own experience of growing knowledge of the Lord. He met Jesus for the first time as a very young man, maybe even a teenager. He was captivated by this Jesus: his healing, his teaching, his interaction with individual people, his love for everyone he met. Then, even after Jesus left his disciples, John thought about him over the years. How could he not when he was caring for Jesus' mother Mary? John meditated on all the words and deeds of Jesus, and over the years, he began to see many layers of deeper meaning in it all. Now John was an old man, perhaps in his eighties or even older, and his knowledge of Jesus was still growing through the indwelling Holy Spirit. The same thing will be true for every follower of Jesus Christ. Our knowledge of him will grow over the years.

Furthermore, it is not simply an intellectual knowledge of Jesus that grows in our minds, it is our personal acquaintance with Jesus and his ways that grows in our hearts, in our souls. William Barclay wrote about this:

> For the Jew knowledge was not merely an intellectual thing. To know God was not merely to know him as the philosopher knows him, it was to know him as a friend knows him. In Hebrew to know is used of the relationship between husband and wife and especially of the sexual act, the most intimate of all relationships.... When John spoke of the increasing knowledge of God, he did not mean that the Christian would become an ever more learned theologian; he meant that throughout the years he would become more and more intimately friendly with God.

The third gift John reminds us about is *strength*. "I write to you, young men, because you are strong, and the word of God lives in you, and you have overcome the evil one."

God gives strength to every Christian through his word living in us. When we think of God's word living in us, we may think of Jesus whom John calls the Word in the prologue to his Gospel. Jesus, the Word, lives in us through his Holy Spirit. This process of Jesus living and growing in us is also aided by our reading, our hearing, and our application of God's word in Scripture. That was how Jesus himself conquered the evil one. Jesus met every temptation in the wilderness by saying to Satan, "It is written...." We can meet and conquer Satan in the same way.

These are three great words of encouragement John gives to us: we are forgiven, we know the Lord, we are strong and can overcome the evil one by the power of God's indwelling word.

I wonder what words of encouragement the Lord may want you and me to speak to others this day? Charles Swindoll wrote the following on this topic some years ago....

> On May 24, 1965, a thirteen-and-a-half-foot boat quietly slipped out of the marina at Falmouth, Massachusetts. Its destination? England. It would be the smallest craft ever to make the voyage. Its name? Tinkerbelle. Its pilot? Robert Manry, a copy editor for the Cleveland Plain Dealer, who felt ten years at the desk was enough boredom for a while, so he took a leave of absence to fulfill his secret dream.
>
> Manry was afraid, not of the ocean, but of all those people who would try to talk him out of the trip. So he didn't share it with many, just some relatives and especially his wife, Virginia. She was his greatest source of support.

The trip? Anything but pleasant. He spent sleepless nights trying to cross shipping lanes without getting run down and sunk. Weeks at sea caused his food to become tasteless. Loneliness, that age-old monster of the deep, led to terrifying hallucinations. His rudder broke three times. Storms swept him overboard, and had it not been for the rope he had knotted around his waist, he would never have been able to pull himself back on board. Finally, after seventy-eight days alone at sea, he sailed into Falmouth, England.

During those nights at the tiller, he had fantasized about what he would do once he arrived. He expected simply to check into a hotel, eat dinner alone, then the next morning see if, perhaps, the Associated Press might be interested in his story. Was he in for a surprise!

Word of his approach had spread far and wide. To his amazement, three hundred vessels, with horns blasting, escorted Tinkerbelle into port. Forty thousand people stood screaming and cheering him to shore. Robert Manry, copy editor turned dreamer, became an overnight hero.

His story has been told around the world. But Robert couldn't have done it alone. Standing on the dock was an even greater hero: Virginia. Refusing to be rigid when Robert's dream was taking shape, she allowed him freedom to pursue his dream.[12]

God's light is seen in God's commands. God's greatest command is love. Thus, God's light is seen when Christians live out a life of love. One of the greatest ways we live out a life of love is through speaking words of encouragement, as Virginia did to her husband. Who is there in your life to whom you might speak words of encouragement today?

Something Not to Love

The United States does not always come in first place. A few years ago, UNICEF surveyed twenty-one of the most developed nations and measured how kids related to other kids, spent time with parents, used alcohol and/or drugs, and perceived their own happiness. Tight-knit nations—like Sweden, the Netherlands, Denmark, and Finland—ranked the highest when it came to young people feeling secure and happy. The U.S. came in next to last, with the United Kingdom at the bottom of the list. UNICEF'S operating thesis was that "stable, supportive family and social relationships are far more important to kids' well being than how much expensive junk they have piled up in their rooms."

William Falk of *The Week* magazine editorialized on these findings:

> It would be comforting to shrug off the report as pure anti-American bunkum. But as the parent of a teen and a tween, I cannot. I've seen firsthand the emptiness that haunts so many middle-class kids. From an early age, they are taught that life is a pitiless pursuit of individual gratification and success, requiring above-average brains and above-average looks. There is no sense of context, or community, or higher purpose. It's hardly surprising that so many of them are taking antidepressants, ADHD meds, or other pills. Many more hide their sadness in eating disorders, drugs, or meaningless hookups. In our rush to give our children everything, I'm afraid, we have forgotten to help them answer a question that won't be ignored: *What is this all for?*[13]

To use a Scriptural phrase, our problem is that we have spent our money on bread that does not satisfy. Thankfully, in 1 John 2:15-17, we are presented with an alternative....

> Do not love the world nor the things in the world. If anyone loves the world, the love of the Father is not in him. For all that is in the world, the lust of the flesh and the lust of the eyes and the boastful pride of life, is not from the Father, but is from the world. The world is passing away, and also its lusts; but the one who does the will of God lives forever. (NASB)

In order to understand this passage properly and apply it in our lives, we must first understand the meaning of several key words in this passage.

The first word we must examine is the word "love". The Greek word here is one you have probably heard about before. It is *agape*. In his book *Love Has Its Reasons*, Earl Palmer explains the background to this important word....

> *Agape* is a word used only sparingly in classical Greek. In fact, the noun form has been found in only four separate places in all of the known classical Greek writings.... In a general sense, *agape* comes close to meaning "good will."
>
> The New Testament writers ... seized hold of this bland, little-known, imprecise word *agape* and loaded it with their own meaning.... *Agape*, then, derives its definition from the Old Testament view of God's strong and faithful love, and from its function in the New Testament text, not from Greek culture and thought.

The Analytical Greek Lexicon defines the verb form of *agape* in this way: "to love, value, esteem, feel or manifest general concern for, be faithful towards, to delight in, to set store upon." *Agape* describes God's unconditional love for humanity.

In his book *Hidden in Plain Sight*, author and pastor Mark Buchanan writes about a woman named Regine. Regine was from Rwanda and came to faith in Jesus Christ while reading her sister's Bible during the genocide that ravaged her country. When she fled to Canada for refuge, she met her husband, Gordon. They decided to return to Rwanda to show the love of Christ to the people who had once been her enemies. Regine told Mark Buchanan this story of *agape* love:

> A woman's only son was killed. She was consumed with grief and hate and bitterness. "God," she prayed, "reveal my son's killer."
>
> One night she dreamed she was going to heaven. But there was a complication: in order to get to heaven she had to pass through a certain house. She had to walk down the street, enter the house through the front door, go through its rooms, up the stairs, and exit through the back door.
>
> She asked God whose house this was.
>
> "It's the house," he told her, "of your son's killer."
>
> The road to heaven passed through the house of her enemy.
>
> Two nights later, there was a knock at her door. She opened it, and there stood a young man. He was about her son's age.
>
> "Yes?"

He hesitated. Then he said, "I am the one who killed your son. Since that day, I have had no life. No peace. So here I am. I am placing my life in your hands. Kill me. I am dead already. Throw me in jail. I am in prison already. Torture me. I am in torment already. Do with me as you wish."

The woman had prayed for this day. Now it had arrived, and she didn't know what to do. She found, to her own surprise, that she did not want to kill him. Or throw him in jail. Or torture him. In that moment of reckoning, she found she only wanted one thing: a son.

"I ask this of you. Come into my home and live with me. Eat the food I would have prepared for my son. Wear the clothes I would have made for my son. Become the son I lost."

And so he did.[14]

That is agape love.

Now, here is another amazing thing: God tells us there is something we *should not* love. There is something to which we should *not* give our unconditional allegiance. That thing is "the world".

We must examine what John means by "the world". The Greek word John uses is "cosmos". It is the same word that is used in John 3:16. "For God so loved the world (the cosmos), that he gave his only begotten Son, that whosoever believes in him should not perish but have everlasting life."

This raises the question: if God loves the cosmos, why cannot we love it as well? The answer is because the word "cosmos" has different shades of meaning throughout the New Testament. In John 3:16, "cosmos" refers to the human beings that God loves in the world. In 1 John 2:15 it refers to the world system itself that is set against God. God wants us to love the world that he has created. God wants us to love other human beings. In both cases, God wants us to love his creation and individual human beings *without condition*. God wants us to work for the good of creation and other human beings. However, God does not want us to love the world system that is set against him and his purposes.

Once again, John sees matters in black and white. If we give our unconditional allegiance to the world system, then the love of the Father is not in us. We cannot at the same time love God and the world system that is against God.

In his book, *Living Peacefully in a Stressful World*, author Ron Hutchcraft describes a visit to Fort Sumter, in Charleston Harbor, South Carolina:

> As the tour boat approached Fort Sumter, I wondered whether the guides would be dressed in blue or in gray. Sumter had been a Union fort in Confederate territory when the Civil War began. It had changed

hands several times.

We were greeted at the gate by a "soldier" wearing a blue coat and gray pants! This uniform wouldn't have worked very well back in 1861. It would have gotten its wearer shot on both ends![15]

What John tells us is that we cannot simply go on wearing a blue coat and grey pants. We must decide which commander we are going to serve. Will it be the world system, or will it be the Lord Jesus Christ?

John goes on to spell out three major characteristics of what we might call "worldliness": the lust of the flesh, the lust of the eyes, and the pride of life. Let us look at each of these in turn.

First, we must define the word "lust". In Greek, the word is $επιθυμια$. The word means "earnest desire" or to heap desire upon desire. Tom Wright translates this word in 1 John 2:16 as "greedy".

Second, we must define the word "flesh". "Flesh" is not the same as body. John is not talking here about the greedy desires of the body. "Flesh" refers to our sinful nature as human beings. Thus, John is simply saying that the greedy desires of our sinful nature belong to the world, not to God.

What does John mean by the lust of the eyes? Our physical eyes are, obviously, the portals through which we view the world. There is nothing wrong with our physical eyes; God created them. There is nothing wrong with our bodily desires; God created those too. However, when we make the satisfaction of our physical desires, wanting more and more, more than what is necessary of this world's goods, in order to satisfy our physical desires, then there is a problem.

Finally, John designates a third characteristic of worldliness that he calls: "the pride of life". The word in the Greek means boasting. Furthermore, the word for "life" is $βιος$; $βιοσ$ refers to physical life as opposed to $ζοε$ that stands for the spiritual life. Thus, the pride of life refers to boasting about all the things of this physical life, boasting of what one has and does.

Tom Wright sums up the meaning of this passage in this way:

> So the command 'not to love the world' refers not to the physical stuff of this world, but to 'the world' as it is in rebellion against God: 'the world' as the combination of things that draw us away from God. The flesh, the eyes, life itself—all can become idols, and like all idols they demand more and more from those who worship them.... We must celebrate all the goodness of the world, all God's goodness to us within his creation. But we must not worship it. We must thank God for it—and pray and watch for the day when it will be transformed by the royal appearing of his son.

A favorite movie of our family in recent years is entitled *The Devil Wears*

Prada. The movie tells the story of Andrea Sachs (played by Anne Hathaway), a journalism graduate who takes a job as second assistant at a prestigious fashion magazine, *Runway*. Caring nothing for fashion, Andrea finds herself working for Miranda Priestly (played by Meryl Streep), the ultra-demanding, diva-like editor of *Runway*. Andrea not only survives, but she begins to thrive in her role; she changes in both appearance and values. She even manages to outperform and outmaneuver the more tenured first assistant, Emily.

Near the end of the film, Andrea has to face up to her transformation, and she does not like what she sees. In one scene, Miranda and Andrea are riding through the streets of Paris after a recent fashion conference that saw Miranda stifle the career of a loyal coworker, Nigel, in order to bolster her own career. Both women are well dressed. Miranda, wearing a fur coat, holds sunglasses in her gloved hand.

"I never thought I would say this, Andrea, but I really…" Miranda pauses and turns to Andrea with a look of pride. "I see a great deal of myself in you. You can see beyond what people want and what they need, and you can choose for yourself."

Andrea shakes her head in disagreement. "I don't think I'm like that." She looks away and continues, "I couldn't do what you did to Nigel, Miranda. I couldn't do something like that."

"You already did. To Emily."

"That's not what I…no, that was different," Andrea says defensively. "I didn't have a choice."

"No, no, you chose. You chose to get ahead. You want this life. Those choices are necessary."

"But what if…this isn't what I want? What if I don't want to live the way you live?"

"Oh, don't be ridiculous, Andrea. Everybody wants this. Everybody wants to be us."

Miranda puts on her sunglasses, smiles, and exits the limo to face a crowd of photographers.[16]

The movie provides a keen depiction of the pull of this world system on even the most ordinary person. Not a one of us is immune to the lust of the flesh, the lust of the eyes, and the pride of life.

However, after all this, you still may be asking: but why does God not want us to love the world? What is so dangerous about the world anyway?

Your reaction to this chapter may be very much like my response when I first committed my life to follow Jesus Christ. I was thirteen years old. I "went forward" in response to an "altar call" at Calvary Memorial Church, a congregation whose building was situated at the corner of one of the busiest intersections in Philadelphia: Roosevelt and Cottman. A man named Dr. Daugherty, a layman in the church, took me aside into a Sunday school room with windows looking out on the bustling city life. The only thing I remember that Dr. Daugherty said to me that day was this.... Pointing out through the windows to the city beyond he said, "This world has nothing to offer you." At the time I thought, but did not say out loud: "This world must have something to offer me."

That may be your reaction today. Why does God not want us to love the world? Personally, I like the way C. S. Lewis answers this question. In a sermon entitled *The Weight of Glory* Lewis says,

> It would seem that Our Lord finds our desires not too strong, but too weak. We are half-hearted creatures, fooling about with drink and sex and ambition when infinite joy is offered us, like an ignorant child who wants to go on making mud pies in a slum because he cannot imagine what is meant by the offer of a holiday at the sea. We are far too easily pleased.

The reason God wants us not to set our affections upon, or fall in love with, this world system, is because God has so much more to offer us. John puts it this way, "The world is passing away, and also its lusts; but the one who does the will of God lives forever." In other words: Why hitch your wagon to a train engine that will not take you to your final destination? Why invest in that which will not last, especially when God promises you a life that will go on forever, each moment better than the one before? Why spend your money for that which is not bread?

In 1 Corinthians 2:9, Paul, quoting Isaiah 64:4 puts forward a startling promise,

> No eye has seen,
> no ear has heard,
> no mind has conceived
> what God has prepared for those who love him.

Given the wonder, the glory, the beauty and richness of this world that God has created, and the amazing imaginative abilities God has given to human beings, that sounds like a fantastic promise to me, one of which I do not want to miss the fulfillment.

The question in the end is this: will we choose to set our affections on this world system, which is but a corrupt version of God's good gift, or will we fall in love with the God who promises us forever? The choice is ours.

Warning about the Anti-Christ

San Francisco and New York City both use a highly efficient system to detect the presence of toxins in their city water supply, toxins that may be a possible sign of a terrorist attack. The two cities have found that the best tool for monitoring such threats are bluegills, those little fish many people catch on a lazy summer afternoon.

According to an article by the Associated Press, these two cities keep a small number of bluegills in a tank at the bottom of their water treatment plants because bluegills are highly attuned to chemical imbalances in their environment. When a disturbance is present in the water, the bluegills react against it. If the computerized system of the treatment plant detects even the slightest change in a bluegill's vital signs, it sends out an e-mail alert.

Bill Lawler, the co-founder of the corporation that makes and sells these bluegill monitoring systems, said, "Nature's given us pretty much the most powerful and reliable early warning center out there."[17]

Just as we need early warning systems to detect potential physical danger, so also we need an early warning system to help us detect spiritual danger. Thankfully, we have just such a system. John tells us about it in 1 John 2:18-23....

> Children, it is the last hour! As you have heard that antichrist is coming, so now many antichrists have come. From this we know that it is the last hour. They went out from us, but they did not belong to us; for if they had belonged to us, they would have remained with us. But by going out they made it plain that none of them belongs to us. But you have been anointed by the Holy One, and all of you have knowledge. I write to you, not because you do not know the truth, but because you know it, and you know that no lie comes from the truth. Who is the liar but the one who denies that Jesus is the Christ? This is the antichrist, the one who denies the Father and the Son. No one who denies the Son has the Father; everyone who confesses the Son has the Father also. (NRSV)

John begins this section of his letter by saying, "Children, it is the last hour." This idea of the last hour or the last days runs throughout Scripture.

The phrase occurs in Genesis 49:1 when Jacob gathers his sons around him before his death to tell them what will happen to them at the "end of the days". In this context, the "end of the days" referred to the time when the people of Israel would enter the Promised Land.

The prophets also used this phrase. In Isaiah 2:2 we read,

> Now it will come about that
> In the last days
> The mountain of the house of the Lord
> Will be established as the chief of the mountains,
> And will be raised above the hills;
> And all the nations will stream to it.

Thus, in the last days, God's holy city will be supreme, and not only Israel, but also all the nations, will gather there.

The last days became associated also with the Day of the Lord. In Joel 3:14 we read, "Multitudes, multitudes in the valley of decision! For the day of the Lord is near in the valley of decision."

William Barclay explains, "The Jews had come to believe that all time was divided into two ages. In between this present age, which was wholly evil, and the age to come, which was the golden time of God's supremacy there was the Day of the Lord, the last days, which would be a time of terror, of cosmic dissolution and of judgment, the birthpangs of the new age."

This does not mean that the Jews envisioned a time of total annihilation of creation. Rather, the Day of the Lord, or the last days, was the time in between this age and a new, perfect age to come. The question is: to which age will we belong? The choice is ours: we can invest in this age that is passing away, along with all of its desires, or we can invest our time, talent and treasure in the age to come. For the early Christians, the whole matter was to be decided in one's response to Jesus.

Now, John felt that the very last hour of the last days was upon God's people. However, two thousand years have passed since that time. Was John wrong?

No, he was not wrong, when you consider that: every person should look at every hour as, potentially, the last. In every hour of every day, there is a conflict raging between good and evil. Will we make the choice for that which is against Christ, or that which is for him?

Even non-Christians realize the importance of looking at each day as, potentially, their last day. Steve Jobs, the founder of Apple who died in 2011, wrote this shortly before his death….

Reflections on 1 John

> When I was 17, I read a quote that went something like: "If you live each day as if it was your last, someday you'll most certainly be right." It made an impression on me, and since then, for the past 33 years, I have looked in the mirror every morning and asked myself: "If today were the last day of my life, would I want to do what I am about to do today?" And whenever the answer has been "No" for too many days in a row, I know I need to change something.
>
> Remembering that I'll be dead soon is the most important tool I've ever encountered to help me make the big choices in life. Because almost everything—all external expectations, all pride, all fear of embarrassment or failure—these things just fall away in the face of death, leaving only what is truly important. Remembering that you are going to die is the best way I know to avoid the trap of thinking you have something to lose. You are already naked.[18]

Of course, the Christian must ask more than simply, "If today were my last day, would I want to be doing this or that?" The Christian must ask, "How will this or that agenda item look in the light of eternity with Christ?" That is a much bigger issue.

Thus, the first key concept that John introduces in this passage is that of "the last hour". The second key concept he touches on is that of the antichrist.

The word "antichrist" can either mean the opponent of Christ or one who puts himself in the place of Christ. The one works by open opposition from the outside, the other by subtle infiltration from within the Church.

The word "antichrist" appears only in the letters of John in the New Testament, but it reflects a very old idea. In the Babylonian legend of creation there is a sea monster called Tiamat that is subdued by the god Marduk. The Israelites took over this idea and the Hebrew Scriptures call this sea monster Rahab. (Job 26:12; Psalm 89:10; Isaiah 51:9)

The Israelites conceived of this evil power as a dragon or serpent. However, over the course of time, the Jews saw this evil as concentrated in particular historical figures like Antiochus Epiphanes, King of Syria, who conquered Israel and set up an altar to Zeus in the Temple in Jerusalem. Daniel refers to this act as the abomination of desolation (Daniel 11:31; 12:11).

Mark uses this same phrase. "But when you see the abomination of desolation standing where it should not be (let the reader understand), then those who are in Judea must flee to the mountains." (Mark 13:14) This reference in Mark, as well as the parallel references in Matthew and Luke, may point to the destruction of Jerusalem and the Temple by the Roman general Titus in AD 70.

Then, in 2 Thessalonians 2:3-4 we read:

> Let no one in any way deceive you, for it will not come unless the apostasy comes first, and the man of lawlessness is revealed, the son of destruction, who opposes and exalts himself above every so-called god or object of worship, so that he takes his seat in the temple of God, displaying himself as being God.

Then, of course, the book of Revelation talks about a beast, probably a representation of Nero who persecuted the early Christians savagely. Down through history, people have fingered various historical figures as the antichrist: Napoleon, Mussolini, Hitler, and Gorbachev among others.

However, according to John, the antichrist is not so much a person as a principle. He tells his readers that many antichrists have already come. To John, the sign that the antichrist, or the spirit of antichrist, is in the world is the existence of false beliefs like those of the Gnostics. Thus, John thought of the antichrist not as one person, but as a spirit of false teaching broadly present in movements that opposed the truth. We will look more specifically at the key truth John was defending in a few moments.

This much is clear, for John, the battle between good and evil was a battle for the mind. This same battle for the mind continues today. I can see it in terms of my own field of publishing. It never ceases to astonish me how many books are published in a given year. In addition to books in print, now we have electronic books of various kinds. I can download a book on almost any subject in the comfort of my own home.

Of course, books are no longer the dominant means of communication. The Internet, accessed through laptop computers and iPads and iPods, probably outpaces every other form of communication in the world today. Yet, I wonder, how much of the information conveyed on the Internet is even accurate, or truthful, let alone, helpful. One thing that the Internet is certainly not conducive towards is deep thinking.

Sidney Poitier has written,

> Child psychologists have demonstrated that our minds are actually constructed by these thousands of tiny interactions during the first few years of life. We aren't just what we're taught. It's what we experience during those early years - a smile here, a jarring sound there - that creates the pathways and connections of the brain. We put our kids through fifteen years of quick-cut advertising, passive television watching, and sadistic video games, and we expect to see emerge a new generation of calm, compassionate, and engaged human beings?

The battle for the mind races on at warp speed today compared to the first century. However, the question that John posed two thousand years ago is just as relevant now: will we listen to the Spirit of Christ or that of antichrist?

Reflections on 1 John

The fact that those teaching heretical doctrines in the first century church had departed from the various Christian assemblies, this John takes as a sign of the last hour. Of course, this does not mean that anyone and everyone who leaves a particular Christian assembly is antichrist.

In the first church that I served as pastor, I had the unfortunate experience of seeing a number of people leave our congregation for various reasons. It was so easy to take that experience as a personal rejection and get defensive. Once one gets defensive, it is easy to see those who depart a congregation as being in the wrong, and those who stay as being completely in the right. However, such is not usually the case. C. H. Dodd once wrote, "Membership of the Church is no guarantee that a man belongs to Christ and not to Antichrist." I believe the opposite of that statement is also true, "Lack of membership in a church is no guarantee that a person does not belong to Christ."

This leads to a very important question: how are we to know the truth?

The Nature of Existence was a 2010 documentary that asked and attempted to answer some of life's biggest questions. One of the segments was on truth. One particular scene began with the word "truth" on the screen and a drawing of a man with his fingers crossed behind his back as if he was concealing something. The narrator then asked questions, and various people would answer.

Narrator: Can you define the word truth?

A Hindu cleric, speaking in his native tongue answered: By worshiping God you can find the truth.

A Tao cleric said: Anything that runs counter to Tao will not be truth.

Then the Narrator asked: What is truth?

Bobby Gaylor, a musician, answered: Truth is what people don't want to hear.

Alan F. Segal, professor of religion at Columbia University said: "When somebody claims to know the truth, and claims to be able to tell it to you, the first thing you should do is check to see if you still have your watch, because that's the prelude to getting taken."

Jim Murphy, champion drag racer answered: "I've had a pretty messed up childhood, and God gave me the faith of a small child. I totally believe. It's all in my heart. I know my knower knows there's a God, and he's in charge of everything. I just know that. To me that's faith."

Julia Sweeney, author of *Letting Go of God* said: "In science, you don't use words like truth. You say, 'Closer to truth.'"

Irvin Kershner, director of *Star Wars: The Empire Strikes Back* answered:

"Only art comes close to trying to answer truth."

A 12-year-old child answered: "I think truth is what we're all searching for, isn't it? Even though, sometimes, it's more fun to search for it than actually find it."[19]

Out of the mouths of babes…

How are we to know the truth? How are we to know what teachings come from antichrist and what comes from Christ himself? John answers that question this way:

> But you have been anointed by the Holy One, and all of you have knowledge. I write to you, not because you do not know the truth, but because you know it, and you know that no lie comes from the truth.

We can know the truth because we have an anointing from the Holy One, that is, from the Holy Spirit. The title "Christ" or in Hebrew "Messiah" means "anointed one". Every person who has put their trust in Christ has been anointed or "Messiahed" by him through the indwelling Spirit. The Holy Spirit guides us into all truth.

That is why, as Samuel Johnson said, we do not so much need to be taught, as we simply need to be reminded of the truth. According to John, the youngest, baby Christian, knows enough of the truth to distinguish it from lies.

What is one of the greatest of all lies, according to John? It is the denial of Jesus as the Christ, the Messiah, the anointed one. According to John, the person who denies that Jesus is the Christ also loses connection with the Father, with God himself. Why is this the case? This is true because, as Jesus himself says in John 14:7, "I am the way, and the truth, and the life; no one comes to the Father except by me."

This does not mean that truth cannot be found in other religions, or that all who follow other religions are certainly lost. However, this does mean that the only hope of salvation comes through acknowledging who Jesus was and is. We as Christians, who share the anointing of Christ, have a tremendous message to share with the entire world: it is the message of God's love embodied in Jesus Christ. We, despite our sin, can connect with a holy God, and it can happen through Jesus. What wonderful good news we have to share!

The late psychiatrist, M. Scott Peck, wrote a book many years ago entitled *People of the Lie*. In the book, Peck discussed actual case histories of people he had counseled in his work, people with extreme dysfunctional behavior. In much of his counseling, Peck said he could track the reasons for his clients' unhappiness and help them toward healing solutions. However, there were some cases where something more sinister seemed to be at work, something that went beyond the normal psychological classifications in which Peck had been trained. All of his training in psychiatry had ruled out use of the E-word. However, through long interaction with various clients, Peck came to belief in the existence of evil.

What was characteristic of these "evil" people was that they were chronic liars. They had lied to themselves and to others, not least to family and friends. What was worse was that these clients were believing and living by their lies. Thereby these clients had invoked the power of the antichrist, the power of the lie, a sort of evil that was more than the sum total of all their own lies put together. This evil power then went to work around these clients with devastating effects. Let me tell you, when I read Peck's book, I read it with all the lights in the house on; it was that scary.

It is just these kind of "people of the lie" that John is warning us against. As N. T. Wright says about John,

> He isn't a psychotherapist; he isn't offering the kind of careful or complex analysis of human motivation that we would expect from a professional in the field today. But he is putting his finger on one great Lie above all, and warning that those who accept this lie and live by it are a corrupting and dangerous influence. Those who do not believe the lie must learn to trust God's work in them, the work because of which they believe the truth. They must hold onto it firmly.

In a world where everyone seems to be talking and very few people are listening, we need to beware that not all messages conform to the truth. Thus, if we want to know the truth we must listen to one voice above every other. I will not say that we need to listen to *only* one voice, because we can find wisdom in many unlikely places. However, we do need to listen to one voice *above* all others: the voice of Jesus.

Staying on Course

There is one thing that I have learned from writing books: it is one thing to start and another thing to finish. There are moments in the middle of the process where I wonder if I will ever reach the end and hold a finished book in my hands. In the muddled middle what is most important is to keep on keeping on.

The same is true in the Christian life: it is relatively easy to start, but hard to continue and cross the finish line. At the beginning of the Christian life, there is the refreshment of forgiveness and the joy of a newfound relationship with Christ. However, in the middle of our journey there are many days when it feels quite difficult to plod on, to keep putting one foot in front of the other. Thus, the key question is: how do we stay on course when we are tempted to drift?

That is the question that John answers for us in 1 John 2:24-29....

> As for you, see that what you have heard from the beginning remains in you. If it does, you also will remain in the Son and in the Father. And this is what he promised us—eternal life.
>
> I am writing these things to you about those who are trying to lead you astray. As for you, the anointing you received from him remains in you, and you do not need anyone to teach you. But as his anointing teaches you about all things and as that anointing is real, not counterfeit—just as it has taught you, remain in him.
>
> And now, dear children, continue in him, so that when he appears we may be confident and unashamed before him at his coming.
>
> If you know that he is righteous, you know that everyone who does what is right has been born of him.

John identifies three closely related steps to staying the course of the Christian life. The first step is: to allow what we have heard from the beginning to remain in us.

Six times in these six verses John uses the same verb, sometimes translated "remain," or "continue," or "abide". The verb appears three times in verse 24 alone. John obviously loves this verb. It means that we need to allow what we have heard from the beginning to take up permanent residence in us, to make a settled home in our hearts.

There are times when we need to go back to the basics of the Christian life and have a refresher course. We do not so much need to be learning new truth, as we need to remember the old truths and put them into practice. That is what John is talking about here.

What are some of the basic truths of the Christian faith that we most need to remember and put into practice? We have mentioned them already in our study of 1 John. I believe that most of all we need to remember:

1. God loves us.
2. God calls us to love him with all of our heart, mind, soul and strength.
3. God calls us to love our neighbors as ourselves.

Think about it. If we just focus on remembering and living out these three truths, we will stay on course in life.

The story is told of Vince Lombardi, coach of the Green Bay Packers, speaking to his team in the locker room after a horrible loss. Lombardi, holding a football aloft said: "Gentlemen, this is a football." Lombardi knew, as any good coach does, when it is time to go back to the basics.

In the Christian life, it is important to review the basics in our minds every day and allow the things that we have heard from the beginning to take up permanent residence in our hearts. God loves us and he wants us to love him and our neighbors as we love ourselves. If we allow these truths that we have heard from the beginning to remain in us, then we will be abiding in the Son, Jesus Christ, and in God the Father. The result of that abiding, both now and after death, will be eternal life.

The second step to staying the course of the Christian life is to allow God's anointing to teach us.

If we want to avoid being led astray by all the false teachings in the world, then John tells us we have to allow God's anointing to teach us. The Greek word translated "to lead astray" is "planao" from which we get our English word "planet". The Greeks contrasted the planets (which they observed as wandering, or as we would say, revolving around the sun) with the stars that remain fixed. In that sense, the anointing of God is like our north star, guiding us amidst all the changes of this life.

As we have seen already in the Hebrew Scriptures, three different types of people were anointed: prophets, priests and kings. Jesus is the fulfillment of all of these. He is our great prophet, priest and king. Therefore, as we abide in Jesus, as we live in him and as he lives in us, we share in his anointing. The anointing is no longer limited to a few special people, the great prophets, priests and kings of the Old Testament. God's anointing now is for all believers in Jesus.

When and how do we receive this anointing? John may be referring to the anointing that comes to the Christian via the Holy Spirit at baptism. (Acts 8:17) The anointing is also connected with the initial teaching that the Christian receives (1 John 2:24, 27). We must always remember that the anointing of the Holy Spirit works through the Word. Thus, there are two tests by which we can judge any new teaching or any decision we must make in life: is it in accord with the teaching of God's Word, and is it in accord with the witness of the Spirit within us?

While I was writing this chapter, the Cardinals of the Catholic Church elected a new pope. Every pope is anointed with oil when he becomes a bishop. Furthermore, all of us have a tendency, whether Catholic or not, to look to the Pope, or to a bishop, or a priest, or a minister, or some preacher on television as having a special anointing from God. While it may be true that the Lord anoints different people for different, special purposes, what John is telling us is that all of us as Christians have an anointing from God, through the Holy Spirit. Therefore, while we can and in fact need to learn much from other teachers in the Lord, we each as Christians have within us an anointing from God that teaches us and guides us.

Thus, the first step to staying the course of the Christian life is to allow those things which we have heard from the beginning to remain in us. The second step is to allow God's anointing to teach us, and the third step is to simply abide in Christ.

John urges us to abide continually in Christ. If we do this, then we will be ready for Jesus when he comes again.

John, here, is recalling the teaching of Jesus in John 15:5. "I am the vine; you are the branches. If you remain in me and I in you, you will bear much fruit; apart from me you can do nothing."

How do we abide in Christ? How do we stay connected to him? We have already spoken about one way that we do that—by allowing the teaching of Jesus to abide in our hearts. We need to read and think on the Word of God, especially that word contained in the Gospels.

Another way that we abide in Christ is through prayer. Prayer does not always require talking on our part. A very important aspect of prayer is silence and listening. If we are often quiet before the Lord I believe we will hear his voice saying, "This is the way, walk ye in it." (Isaiah 30:21)

A third essential means of grace, or means of abiding in Christ, goes by various names: the Mass, the Eucharist, Holy Communion, or the Lord's Supper. Personally, I like the term: Holy Communion. Through partaking of the bread and of the cup in faith, we truly commune with Christ and stay connected to him.

Then, a fourth important means of grace is the fellowship of God's people.

Reflections on I John

If we are connected to Jesus as a branch to a vine, then we will be connected to all the other branches that are connected to him. We can learn from one another and grow together into a mighty and fruitful plant for the Lord.

This leads to the final point that John makes in this section of his letter. That is that abiding in Christ will manifest itself in righteous living. If we remain connected to the love of Jesus then that love will issue forth from us to others in word and deed. Certainly, the most important way we show the love of Jesus is by our actions.

Anglican priest and author Michael Green shares the following story to remind us of the impact of our actions long before our words. Green says:

> I read about a missionary candidate in language school. The very first day of class the teacher entered the room and, without saying a word, walked down every row of students. Finally, still without saying a word, she walked out of the room again. Then she came back and addressed the class. "Did you notice anything special about me?" she asked.
>
> Nobody could think of anything in particular. One student finally raised her hand. "I noticed that you had on a very lovely perfume," she said. The class chuckled.
>
> But the teacher said, "That was exactly the point. [It] will be a long time before any of you will be able to speak Chinese well enough to share the gospel with anyone in China. But even before you are able to do that, you can minister the sweet fragrance of Christ to these people by the quality of your lives."[20]

The new pope has very intriguingly taken the name of Francis. He is the first pope to ever bear that name. His namesake, St. Francis of Assisi, is reported to have said these classic words: "Preach the Gospel at all times; if necessary, use words."

Paul puts it this way in 2 Corinthians 2:15-16,

For we are to God the pleasing aroma of Christ among those who are being saved and those who are perishing. To the one we are an aroma that brings death; to the other, an aroma that brings life.

What kind of fragrance do you spread abroad in the lives of others? Is it an aroma of life or of death? If we abide in Christ, if we stay connected to him at all times by allowing his word to remain in us and his anointing to teach us, then we will spread the sweet aroma of his love wherever we go.

Living in God's Family

In an article in *Christianity Today* several years ago, Bill Glass wrote:

> What is our country's biggest problem? A lack of a father's blessing. The FBI studied the 17 kids who shot their classmates in towns like Paducah, Kentucky; Pearl, Mississippi; and Littleton, Colorado. All 17 shooters had only one thing in common: they had a father problem. I see it so much; it's just unbelievable. There's something about it when a man doesn't get along with his father. It makes him mean; it makes him dangerous; it makes him angry.
>
> On the day before Father's Day, I was in North Carolina in a juvenile prison. I ate lunch with three boys. I asked the first boy, "Is your dad coming to see you tomorrow on Father's Day?"
>
> He said, "No, he's not coming."
>
> "Why not?" I asked.
>
> "He's in prison."
>
> I asked the second boy the same question and got the same answer. I asked the third one why his dad wasn't coming, and he said: "He got out of prison about nine months ago, and he's doing good, and I'm proud of my father. He's really going to be a good dad to me, and he's going to go straight."
>
> I could tell he was protesting so strongly because something was still wrong. So I said, "How many times has he been here to see you since he got out nine months ago?"
>
> He said, "He hasn't made it out yet."
>
> "Why not?"
>
> "Well, he lives way, way away."
>
> "Where does he live?"
>
> "He lives in Durham."
>
> Durham was only two hours away. I had come 1,500 miles to visit the boy. His dad couldn't come two hours? There are a lot of fathers who

are really deserters. When I'm in a prison, I always challenge inmates to bless their kids. If you want to keep your kids out of prison, bless them.[21]

In a world that desperately needs the love of a father, we have some wonderfully good news to share. We read about that good news in 1 John 3:1-6....

> See what great love the Father has lavished on us, that we should be called children of God! And that is what we are! The reason the world does not know us is that it did not know him. Dear friends, now we are children of God, and what we will be has not yet been made known. But we know that when Christ appears, we shall be like him, for we shall see him as he is. All who have this hope in him purify themselves, just as he is pure.
>
> Everyone who sins breaks the law; in fact, sin is lawlessness. But you know that he appeared so that he might take away our sins. And in him is no sin. No one who lives in him keeps on sinning. No one who continues to sin has either seen him or known him.

There are three important things that John tells us here about living in God's family. First, we have a relationship of love with the Father.

What sort of love is this? John uses the Greek word ποταπος when he says: "See *what sort of* love the Father has given us!" Ποταπος literally means "of what country". Greeks used this word to express surprise when they encountered something foreign. The disciples used this word in Matthew 8:27 when Jesus calmed the storm on the Sea of Galilee and they asked, "What kind of man is this? Even the winds and the waves obey him!" Jesus was in a different category altogether from anything or anyone that the disciples had come across before. The same is true of the Father's love for us: it is in an entirely different category from any other love.

God reveals his amazing love for us by calling us his children. Now, you may wonder: why is this so amazing? Is not everyone created by God and therefore his child? The answer from the Bible is both yes and no. William Barclay explains our situation in this way:

> It is by the gift of God that a man becomes a child of God. By nature a man is the creature of God, but it is by grace that he becomes the child of God. There are two English words which are closely connected but whose meanings are widely different, paternity and fatherhood. Paternity describes a relationship in which a man is responsible for the physical existence of a child; fatherhood describes an intimate, loving, relationship. In the sense of paternity all men are children of God; but in the sense of fatherhood men are children of God only when he

makes his gracious approach to them and they respond.

The Apostle Paul calls this gracious approach on God's part "adoption". In Romans 8:15-17 he writes,

> For you did not receive a spirit of slavery to fall back into fear, but you have received a spirit of adoption. When we cry, "Abba! Father!" it is that very Spirit bearing witness with our spirit that we are children of God, and if children, then heirs, heirs of God and joint heirs with Christ.

Naturally, the question arises: if Christians are children of God why does the rest of the world not recognize this truth? The answer is: because we are receiving the same treatment Jesus received. The world did not recognize Jesus as the Son of God; therefore, the world will not recognize us for who we really are either.

An episode of the TV show *Parenthood* focused on a couple's attempt to adopt a young Hispanic boy named Victor. After living with the Graham family for a while, Victor began to open his heart to Joel and Julia, but then he suddenly drew back again. He refused to eat meals with his family; he fought with his future sister, and Victor expressed hatred to Julia, his future mother.

Julia was afraid that Victor would never return her love and she began to doubt the decision to finalize the adoption. At one point, she told her brother Crosby: "We've had all this time together, and it just doesn't seem like we're progressing.... He just doesn't like me. At this point, it's so hard to know that that's gonna change.... [maybe] I shouldn't be his mom."

Later in the show, Julia explains to Victor, "[We're] going to choose a date next week to finalize your adoption. You know what that means?"

"Not really," Victor replies.

Julia says, "That means we're gonna go to court, all of us together, and we're gonna stand in front of a judge and we will promise to take care of you. And we'll probably sign some papers and we'll be your mom and dad from now on. Does that sound good to you?"

Victor says "Sure" even though it is clear he does not understand what adoption means.

Then, in the next episode, Victor finally understands it all. As he is racing through the house playing football, Victor accidentally smashes an expensive vase. When Julia races into the room, Victor says, "I'm sorry. I'll pay for it."

"It's okay, you don't have to pay for it," says Julia. "Let's just go back to the no-football-in-the-house rule."

Victor then asks, "So you're not going to change your mind about adopting me?"

Julia responds, "No. I'm never gonna change my mind."

Unable to wipe the smile off his face, Victor responds, "Okay." From that point forward, the knowledge of his adoption and of his parents' unconditional love helps Victor to bond with his new family.[22]

The same is true in our relationship with God. He has adopted us as his sons and daughters through Jesus Christ, and he is not ever going to go back on that decision. At present, the world may not recognize to whom we belong. However, we know, and we can relax in our heavenly Father's love.

Thus, the first major thing John tells us about living in God's family is that we have a relationship of love with our heavenly father. The second major thing John tells us is that God has given us a hope that purifies.

What is that hope? John tells us that we are already the children of God; it is a present fact. However, what we will be in the future has not yet been revealed. There is a "now but not yet" aspect to the Christian life. We have many blessings from God in the present, but he has so much more in store for us.

Despite not knowing much about our future state, what the resurrection life will be like, John is sure of two things. *First, when Jesus appears we will be like him.*

John is most likely thinking all the way back to Genesis 1:27....

> So God created humankind in his image,
> in the image of God he created them;
> male and female he created them.

However, in between where we are now and Genesis chapter one there is Genesis chapter three: the story of the fall of humankind from God's original, intended perfection. What John is telling us is that in Jesus we will recover that original perfection, the image of God.

The first point John makes here relates to the second. *That is: when Jesus appears we shall see him as he is.*

There was a man who had gone blind as a young adult. Subsequently, the man married and had children. His family could see him, but he had never seen them. Then, through the miracle of medicine, the man was able to have an operation and he regained his eyesight. What a wonderful moment that must have been, after the operation, to open his eyes and see his wife and children for the first time! Perhaps, in a way, our vision of Jesus in the resurrection life will be like that.

One thing is certain: something about eye contact changes us. People who spend a lifetime looking at each other begin to look *like* each other. Perhaps that is because we unconsciously copy the facial expressions of those we love until that experience actually reshapes the muscles in our faces. John tells us that something of the same thing is going to happen through the long journey of the Christian life that Paul calls sanctification.

The story is told of a poor man who often went into a cathedral to pray. He would pray, kneeling before the crucifix. His lips never moved. It appeared that he never said a single word. An observer asked the man about his prayer practice. The poor man described it by pointing to Jesus on the cross and saying: "I look at him; and he looks at me."

I think what John is telling us is that the person who looks long enough at Jesus will become like him. Furthermore, when we become completely like Jesus we will really see him as he is for the first time.

This leads to the final major point that John makes about living in God's family. As we spend our lives gazing at Jesus, there will be a reflection of the Father in our lifestyle. If we have the hope that we will one day see Jesus face to face, and that in that day we will become completely like him, then we will want to get busy on that journey of becoming like him here and now.

It is like this…. If you were going to meet a colleague in some other country at some time in the not too distant future, then you would want to learn as much of that colleague's language as possible, so that when the two of you did meet, you could converse more freely.

To use another illustration, imagine that one day you read about your dream job in the classified ads of the newspaper. What would you do then? You would call up the company and make an appointment for an interview. Then, you would learn everything you possibly could about that company, and gear everything in your resume toward what that company was looking for in an employee. You would do this so that when the day of the interview arrived, you would make the best impression possible.

In the same way, John tells us that one day we are going to meet Jesus. Now Jesus is perfectly pure, holy, set apart. If we want to properly prepare for that meeting, we will start working now at making ourselves pure by the power of the Holy Spirit whom Jesus has given to us.

How do we do that? In answer to that question, John tells us something that at first sight seems very troublesome: "No one who lives in him [that is in Jesus] keeps on sinning."

What does John mean? If we share in the life of Jesus, if we live in him and Jesus lives in us, then we will live changed lives. John recognizes that none of us will be completely free of sin until that day that we stand before Jesus and see him as he is, for in that day we will be made like him. John has already told us at the end of chapter one and the beginning of chapter two what to do when sin crops up in our lives: confess it and receive forgiveness through Jesus. What John is talking about here is that the Christian does not live in sin as a habit of life.

N. T. Wright describes this daily process of transformation in this way:

We should be doing our best to avoid all kinds of sin, all the time, though we shall surely fail; but the failures must take place within a settled habit of life in which sin is no longer setting the tone. We are playing a different piece of music now, and even if our fingers slip sometimes and play some wrong notes, notes that belong to the music we used to play, that doesn't mean we are going back to play that old music for real once more.

Therefore, we are not talking about achieving an unrealistic standard of total perfection in our day-to-day living. The question is: how do we start playing more of the right notes from the score Jesus wants us to play and fewer of the wrong notes that belong to our old sinful lifestyle? The secret is to *abide in Jesus*. "No one who abides in him keeps on sinning."

This statement takes us back, once again, to the language of Jesus in the Gospel of John, chapter fifteen, where Jesus says:

> I am the true vine, and my Father is the vinegrower.... Abide in me as I abide in you. Just as the branch cannot bear fruit by itself unless it abides in the vine, neither can you unless you abide in me. I am the vine, you are the branches. Those who abide in me and I in them bear much fruit, because apart from me you can do nothing.... If you abide in me, and my words abide in you, ask for whatever you wish, and it will be done for you.... As the Father has loved me, so I have loved you; abide in my love. (NRSV)

We abide in Jesus by allowing his word to abide in us, by filling our minds and hearts with his words. We abide in Jesus by talking to him in prayer: "ask whatever you wish, and it will be done for you." We abide in Jesus by abiding in his love, by receiving that love, soaking ourselves in it, and relishing it.

If we attempt merely to keep sin at bay by our own power, to try to hold something out by brute strength, we will surely fail. Rather, what we need to do is let the larger life of Jesus seep into us day by day.

When you put a tea bag in hot water, slowly the flavor and color of that tea disperses throughout that cup or mug of water. Just so, we need to let the flavor and color of the life of Jesus steep in us. If we do that, then in time there will be no more room for our old way of life, for mere, bland, tasteless, hot water.

As we abide in Jesus, not only will the room for sin gradually decrease in our lives, but we will also be able to handle any stress that hits us from the outside.

Allow me to close with a little story that illustrates this so well. When I tell people I am from California, non-Californians often reply: "I could never live there. I would be afraid of the earthquakes." One of my favorite preachers who served for many years in Berkeley California, Earl Palmer, gives an excellent response to this fear. He writes...

> I want to tell you something that may surprise you. If you're making a trip to San Francisco and you want the safest place to go, you go to the middle of the Golden Gate Bridge. That will withstand probably 9.0 on the Richter Scale. It's a magnificent structure. It will not fall, for two reasons. One, it's flexible. That sway. But I'll tell you another reason it stands: That bridge is a marvel of cantilever and suspension in construction.
>
> Every bit of concrete, and all the macadam and that pavement, and every bit of steel in that entire bridge—all of it relates one piece to another. Every piece of metal in that bridge finally relates to two giant cables, that finally come up to two great piers that go down into bedrock, and two anchors out on each side. That's the genius of a suspension bridge—every single piece of metal, every single piece of concrete, is preoccupied with its foundation. And it's satisfied with the foundation. You don't see big, huge cables going from the top of the bridge over to the Trans-America Tower, or over to redwood trees over in Marin County; you don't have that. They decide to trust the pure living rock that those great piers go into.[23]

When we abide in Jesus and his words abide in us, when we allow our roots to go down deep into the soil of his marvelous love, then we are actually anchored in the Rock, and all the stress, all the sin, and even Satan himself cannot shake us loose.

Who Is A Real Christian?

On a cross-country flight many years ago, I took the opportunity to talk to the businessman seated next to me about Jesus Christ. He was rather unimpressed with most of what I had to say until I told him about my father and my father's work in New York City trying to help teenagers get out of gangs. The courage, the goodness, and selfless service of my father to those far less fortunate than himself, really did impress this particular, hardened, New York businessman.

That is often the way of it. Non-Christians are seldom impressed by what we, as Christians, say; it is what we do that matters to them. John has a similar perspective on the Christian life. Hear what he has to say from 1 John 3:7-10 about who is a real Christian....

> Dear children, do not let anyone lead you astray. The one who does what is right is righteous, just as he is righteous. The one who does what is sinful is of the devil, because the devil has been sinning from the beginning. The reason the Son of God appeared was to destroy the devil's work. No one who is born of God will continue to sin, because God's seed remains in them; they cannot go on sinning, because they have been born of God. This is how we know who the children of God are and who the children of the devil are: Anyone who does not do what is right is not God's child, nor is anyone who does not love their brother and sister.

Who is a real Christian? John offers a four-part response to this very important question. First off, John suggests that the person who does what is right is a real Christian.

John begins this section of his letter by warning his audience, "Dear children, do not let anyone lead you astray." John was probably thinking about the Gnostics whom we have talked about before. They claimed to have a secret "gnosis" or knowledge about Jesus. They claimed to be spiritually superior. Yet, in that superiority, some of them also claimed that it did not matter what they did with their bodies; spirit was all that mattered to the Gnostics.

John's response to this is a resounding "No!" John insists that it *does* matter what we do with our bodies. "The one who does what is right is righteous, just as he is righteous. The one who does what is sinful is of the devil, because the devil has been sinning from the beginning."

Once again, these verses raise a question we have asked before in our study of 1 John. Is John suggesting that the Christian does no wrong? It sounds that way when he says, "No one who is born of God will continue to sin." How does this fit with what John says in 1 John 1:8? "If we claim to be without sin, we deceive ourselves and the truth is not in us."

I think what John is suggesting is that, yes, Christians commit sin; however, Christians do not *live in* sin, they do not commit sin habitually, as a way of life, as something they are satisfied with. That is the big difference: between the person who really knows Christ and the one who does not.

Len Sullivan tells the following story....

> In the late 1920s my grandparents married and moved into Grandpa's old family home. It was a clapboard house with a hall down the middle. In the 30s they decided to tear down the old house and build another to be their home for the rest of their lives.
>
> Much to my grandmother's dismay, many of the materials of the old house were re-used in their new house. They used old facings and doors, and many other pieces of the finishing lumber. Everywhere my grandmother looked, she saw that old house—old doors that wouldn't shut properly, crown molding split and riddled with nail holes, unfinished window trimming. It was a source of grief to her. All her life she longed for a new house.
>
> When God brings us into the kingdom, the old way of living must be dismantled and discarded.[24]

Paul puts it this way in 2 Corinthians 5:17, "Therefore, if anyone is in Christ, the new creation has come: The old has gone, the new is here!"

That does not mean we will not sin and make mistakes as Christians. We do and we will until that day when Jesus perfects us in his presence. However, a new work has begun; a new house is being built with new material, and we are that house!

Now, let us examine what it is that really makes this difference in the life of the Christian. The second major thing John tells us is that the real Christian is one who has Christ working in him to destroy the devil's work.

The word for "destroy" literally means: "to loose, untie, set free". This word is used of untying the donkey that Jesus used to ride into Jerusalem on Palm Sunday, and unwrapping the grave clothes that bound Lazarus before Jesus raised him from the dead. This word was also used of breaking something down into its component parts, or tearing down an old building and so destroying it. What John is telling us is that Jesus came to tear down the old, sinful life that the devil is constantly tempting us to live. Jesus came to set us free.

This raises a question for some people: why does God allow the devil to bring such havoc to our lives anyway? I think the answer to this question is the same as the answer to the question: why did God allow humans to choose evil? The answer is the same, whether we are talking about human beings or angels. C. S. Lewis put the answer this way:

> God created things which had free will. That means creatures which can go either wrong or right. Some people think they can imagine a creature which was free but had no possibility of going wrong; I cannot. If a thing is free to be good it is also free to be bad. And free will is what has made evil possible. Why, then, did God give them free will? Because free will, though it makes evil possible, is also the only thing that makes possible any love or goodness or joy worth having. A world of automata—of creatures that worked like machines—would hardly be worth creating. The happiness which God designs for His higher creatures is the happiness of being freely, voluntarily united to Him and to each other in an ecstasy of love and delight compared with which the most rapturous love between a man and a woman on this earth is mere milk and water. And for that they must be free.[25]

Therefore, free will is what has made the devil possible, and it is what has made our own evil choices possible. The good news is that God has given us a power that can counteract the evil force of the devil. That power is the Holy Spirit living in us.

Clark Cothern writes,

> One of the more humorous quirks of scientific history is the debate over who should get the credit for discovering oxygen. Joseph Priestley, an English scientist and clergyman, is often given that honor because he was the first to publish his findings, doing so in 1774. Interestingly, Priestley originally called the gas, "dephlogisticated air."
>
> However, in 1772, two years prior to Priestly's find, a Swedish chemist named Carl Scheele independently discovered the gas that is vital to human existence. Strangely enough, the term oxygen didn't actually come into use until 1775, when yet another chemist, Frenchman Antoine Lavoisier, discovered and named the gas we breathe. Lavoisier was the first to recognize oxygen as one of our natural elements.
>
> Regardless of who gets the credit, it's odd to think of a human being "discovering" oxygen. Does a fish discover water? The truth is that oxygen literally surrounds us every day, and even if we choose to call it "dephlogisticated air," we can't live without it. The same is true of the Holy Spirit.[26]

John tells us that Jesus came to this world to destroy, to set us free from, the work of the devil. Jesus did that by living for us, by dying on the cross, by rising again, ascending into heaven, and sending us the gift of the Holy Spirit. Paul tells us that the Holy Spirit is like a sword that God gives us to fight against the devil (Ephesians 6:17). That gift of the Spirit, living inside us, is also like oxygen for our souls. The Spirit frees us from the suffocating power of Satan. However you look at the subject, whatever words you use to describe it, the truth is that the real Christian has the power of Christ's Spirit working inside of him or her to destroy the power of the devil.

A third thing John tells us here is that real Christians have God's seed in them.

What is God's seed exactly? What is it that causes us to be "born of God"?

At least twice in the New Testament, we are told that the word of God brings about the new birth. James 1:18 says that God "chose to give us birth through the word of truth, that we might be a kind of firstfruits of all he created," and 1 Peter 1:23 says, "For you have been born again, not of perishable seed, but of imperishable, through the living and enduring word of God." Furthermore, Paul tells us in Ephesians 6:17 that the sword of the Spirit *is* the word of God. Therefore, I believe we can conclude that it is the Holy Spirit, using the word of God, who brings new life to our souls. The real Christian is the one in whom the Holy Spirit is doing this work through the word of God.

Does transformation through the Spirit and the word happen all at once? No, I do not believe so. Rather, it is a gradual process. I like what Bono, the lead singer of the band U2 says about this:

> Your nature is a hard thing to change; it takes time.... I have heard of people who have life-changing, miraculous turnarounds, people set free from addiction after a single prayer, relationships saved where both parties "let go, and let God." But it was not like that for me. For all that "I was lost, I am found," it is probably more accurate to say, "I was really lost. I'm a little less so at the moment." And then a little less and a little less again. That to me is the spiritual life. The slow reworking and rebooting the computer at regular intervals, reading the small print of the service manual. It has slowly rebuilt me in a better image. It has taken years, though, and it is not over yet.[27]

I love that—reworking and rebooting the computer at regular intervals! That is the work of the Holy Spirit. Every day we can choose to let the Holy Spirit have his way with us, to rework and reboot us, and one major way we allow him to work on our souls is by "reading the small print of the service manual"—that is the word of God.

Reflections on I John

A final thing John tells us here about the real Christian is something he is going to say a lot more about in the remainder of his letter, but he gives us a little preview here. John tells us that the real Christian is one who loves his brothers and sisters.

This is how we know who the children of God are and who the children of the devil are: Anyone who does not do what is right is not God's child, nor is anyone who does not love their brother and sister.

A Sunday school teacher was discussing the Ten Commandments with her class of five and six-year-olds. After explaining the commandment to honor thy father and thy mother, she asked, "Is there a commandment that teaches us how to treat our brothers and sisters?"

Without missing a beat, one little boy answered, "Thou shall not kill."[28]

It is true that we sometimes have great difficulty truly loving those closest to us—our brothers and sisters. However, loving our brothers and sisters obviously involves more than just "not murdering them". We need to do positive good unto them as well.

David Jackman writes,

> The righteousness that demonstrates our membership in God's family is not cold and clinical. It is inseparable from love. The God who is light is also love. Love is righteousness in relationship with others—not primarily an emotion, but an act of will. It is not feeling warm toward people in a general way, but doing good to specific individuals. Love as a feeling only is useless. No marriage can survive on feelings. Love has to be expressed in caring and sharing, in hard work and loyalty, in generosity and long-suffering. That's the love without which we have no right to claim to be God's children. Of course it is superhuman. It does not grow naturally in this world's soil. It is the gift of God. But where it exists, there is positive proof of the life of God in the soul of man, and so of authentic membership in God's family.

Who are the brothers and sisters whom we are to love? Certainly, our fellow Christians are our brothers and sisters. However, in a larger way, our fellow human beings are our brothers and sisters as well. We need to always remember Jesus' parable of the Good Samaritan. We should not ask, "Who is my neighbor?" but rather "How can I be a good neighbor to everyone I meet?"

Of course, loving another human being, whether it is our brother or sister in Christ, or if it is simply someone we meet along the road, loving another is the greatest thing we can do in life.

Not long before his death, Martin Luther King Jr. spoke to the congregation at Atlanta's Ebenezer Baptist Church. On that day he said:

> If any of you are around when I have to meet my day, I don't want a long funeral. And if you get somebody to deliver the eulogy, tell them not to talk too long. Every now and then I wonder what I want them to say. Tell them not to mention that I have a Nobel Peace Prize; that isn't important. Tell them not to mention that I have three or four hundred other awards; that's not important. Tell them not to mention where I went to school. I'd like somebody to mention that day that Martin Luther King Jr. tried to love somebody.[29]

Simply loving another human being is the greatest thing any one of us can do.

Okay, so the real Christian is one who does what is right, the one who has the Holy Spirit working in him or her to destroy the work of the devil, one who has the seed of God which is God's word, and the real Christian is one who loves his or her brothers and sisters. However, even when we know all this, the question comes: how am I to live out the life of a real Christian starting on Monday morning? How do I live out real Christianity in a world made up of more than fifty shades of grey?

I like the way Robert Raines answers these questions with this poetic prayer:

> I have to decide Yes or No
> And neither option seems wholly right
> But there is no third possibility
>
> Not to decide is to decide
> So I must decide one way
> Or the other…
> Either way
> Somebody gets hurt
> There's no painless, pure way through
> My hands are tied
> There are limits and I've reached them
> How can I justify what I have to do?
> To the parties involved?
> To myself?
> To you?
>
> Lord, will you go with me
> As I decide?
> Cover my inevitable sin with your grace
> Accept me
> Even when I'm unacceptable

Reflections on I John

Let my Yes or No
Be born out of
A brave trust

Love One Another

If you had to pick one word to describe Christianity, what would that word be? In many ways, John suggests to us that *love* best describes what Christianity is all about: God's love for us, our love for God and, as John points out in this next passage, the love we ought to have for one another. Let's see what he has to say about love in 1 John 3:11-18....

> For this is the message you heard from the beginning: We should love one another. Do not be like Cain, who belonged to the evil one and murdered his brother. And why did he murder him? Because his own actions were evil and his brother's were righteous. Do not be surprised, my brothers and sisters, if the world hates you. We know that we have passed from death to life, because we love each other. Anyone who does not love remains in death. Anyone who hates a brother or sister is a murderer, and you know that no murderer has eternal life residing in him.
>
> This is how we know what love is: Jesus Christ laid down his life for us. And we ought to lay down our lives for our brothers and sisters. If anyone has material possessions and sees a brother or sister in need but has no pity on them, how can the love of God be in that person? Dear children, let us not love with words or speech but with actions and in truth.

In this passage, John tells us about two attitudes, two examples, and two destinations. First, let us look together at the two attitudes John describes.

It has been said that attitude determines altitude. In flying a plane, that is absolutely true. The pitch attitude of the nose of the plane determines whether that plane is going to go up, or down. What is true in flying is also true in everyday life: our attitude will determine our altitude, how high we fly, close to God, or low and far away from him.

John talks about two attitudes in this passage: one is nose up, and it will take us closer to God, the other is nose down and will take us further away from God. The attitude that will move us further away from God is hatred.

John says, "Do not be surprised, my brothers and sisters, if the world hates you." In other words, hatred is the characteristic attitude of this present world system that is set against God. Most people will say that they love other people, but the everyday ups and downs of life will reveal whether this is true or not. The saying is all too true: "I love humankind; it's people I can't stand."

If I am carrying a cup of water that is full to the brim and I bump into someone else then water is going to spill out. The question is: in our everyday lives when we hit bumps, what spills out? How do we habitually react to the knocks and irritations of life? John is telling us that apart from Christ working in us, our natural response to the bumps of life will be hatred. Whatever is in us is what will spill out.

For example, I was with a friend the other day and took him to pick up some shoes that a cobbler was repairing for him. However, when my friend arrived at the shop, he discovered that the cobbler had not even worked on his shoes after having them in his possession for a month or more. My friend was rather irritated and expressed that irritation to me.

Now you may say to me: "But that is a natural response!" I would agree. If I were in the same position I might respond with the same level of irritation as my friend did.

I think that is precisely what John is telling us. Apart from Christ working in us our natural response to the bumps of life, the big ones and the little ones, will be anger, irritation and hatred.

You may say, "Well, that's no big deal." However, John thinks it is a big deal. He says, "Anyone who hates a brother or sister is a murderer, and you know that no murderer has eternal life residing in him."

Furthermore, John is not saying this on his own authority. Jesus said the same thing in Matthew 5....

> You have heard that it was said to the people long ago, "You shall not murder, and anyone who murders will be subject to judgment." But I tell you that anyone who is angry with a brother or sister will be subject to judgment. Again, anyone who says to a brother or sister, 'Raca,' is answerable to the court. And anyone who says, 'You fool!' will be in danger of the fire of hell.

If anger and hatred are such serious problems, then what should we do about them? Thankfully, Jesus gives us an answer, also in Matthew 5....

> Therefore, if you are offering your gift at the altar and there remember that your brother or sister has something against you, leave your gift there in front of the altar. First go and be reconciled to them; then come and offer your gift.
>
> Settle matters quickly with your adversary who is taking you to court. Do it while you are still together on the way, or your adversary may hand you over to the judge, and the judge may hand you over to the

officer, and you may be thrown into prison. Truly I tell you, you will not get out until you have paid the last penny.

Jesus says that when we are angry, when we sense feelings of hatred rising within us, we should deal with our anger quickly and seek reconciliation with our brother or sister. Paul says the same thing....

> In your anger do not sin: Do not let the sun go down while you are still angry, and do not give the devil a foothold. (Ephesians 4:26-27)

This verse makes it clear that anger is not the problem, but rather *what we do with it*. After all, even Jesus was angry and displayed that anger by driving the buyers and the sellers out of the Temple. Of course, in that instance, Jesus was displaying righteous anger, whereas our anger, most of the time, contains a mix of righteous and unrighteous elements. The real problem comes when we allow our anger to develop into a deep-seated hatred of others.

Thus, hatred is the first attitude we see in this passage. It is a "nose down" attitude that will take us away from God unless we deal with it quickly and seek reconciliation.

The second attitude John talks about is love. "For this is the message you heard from the beginning: We should love one another."

Love is the foundation for all genuine Christian spirituality. Love is not merely an occasional practice for God; love is at the very core of God's being. If this is true, and I believe it is, then a person cannot come into relationship with God without simultaneously becoming a more loving human being. This change does not happen all at once. Total change requires a lifetime. However, one can begin to see change in the life of every true Christian.

In response you may ask, "Then why do I know so many non-Christians who are more loving than Christians?" I would have to agree. However, I think there are a few reasons why this appears to be the case.

First off, no one starts out even in life with everyone else. We each enter this world with a certain genetic make-up that predisposes us to certain problems and not others. Second, everyone's experiences are different. Even two children growing up in the same family will experience love, or the lack of it, differently. Thus, if we were to prove somehow scientifically that Christianity always makes people more loving than if they were not Christians, we would have to know everything about the genetics and the nurture of the people under scrutiny. We would have to know not simply something about their external circumstances and appearances, but we would have to know something of their interior life to make a proper judgment. The fact is: we simply cannot know these things and so we cannot make a proper judgment. When we see non-Christian "A" who appears to be more loving than Christian "B" then we must ask: What would non-Christian "A" be like if he or she was a Christian?

Reflections on I John

Would he or she be even more loving than they are now? Furthermore, what would Christian "B" be like if they were not Christian? Would they be even more unloving than they are now? In addition, we cannot really know how Christ may be working in someone's heart. The person who says they are not Christian may actually have more of the spirit of Christ working in them, and the person who says they are Christian may, in fact, know nothing of Jesus in a personal, spiritual manner.

However, let us stop talking about hypothetical examples. Let us go on to examine the two examples that John puts before us. The first one is an example of hatred at work, and his name is Cain.

The story of Cain in the Hebrew Scriptures shows us how hatred often gets to work in the human soul. First off, John says that Cain belonged to the evil one, that is, the devil. Wherever hatred is at work, we can be sure that the devil is present. That does not mean that there is no hope for the person in whom Satan is working, but we can be certain about the source of all hatred.

Second, not only did the evil one influence Cain, but also Cain's own inner jealousy of his brother got the better of him. John tells us that Cain killed his brother because his brother's actions were good and his were evil. What are the actions about which John is talking? If we re-visit the original story in Genesis 4, we find out....

> Now Abel kept flocks, and Cain worked the soil. In the course of time Cain brought some of the fruits of the soil as an offering to the Lord. And Abel also brought an offering—fat portions from some of the firstborn of his flock. The Lord looked with favor on Abel and his offering, but on Cain and his offering he did not look with favor. So Cain was very angry, and his face was downcast.

What was the problem here? Why did God look with favor on Abel's offering and not on Cain's? Was it because Abel brought an animal sacrifice and Cain's sacrifice was merely one of vegetables? I do not think so. I do not believe God ever asks us to give what we do not have. Cain worked the soil, so the natural gift for him to bring to God would be the produce of his garden. I believe the difference between Cain and Abel, and why God looked with favor on one offering and not the other, is because Abel brought the *firstborn* of his flock to God, whereas Cain merely brought his *leftovers*—"some of the fruits of the soil".

Now, notice that Cain was angry because of the way God treated him. He did not have a right to be angry because God dealt with him in perfect justice. However, the thing to see is that disobedience was the first step in Cain's downward spiral, and anger was the second step. Furthermore, God in his grace gave Cain a way out. God said to Cain,

> Why are you angry? Why is your face downcast? If you do what is right, will you not be accepted? But if you do not do what is right, sin is crouching at your door; it desires to have you, but you must rule over it.

God gave to Cain the opportunity to pull out of the downward spiral. However, Cain did not take advantage of that opportunity....

> Now Cain said to his brother Abel, "Let's go out to the field." While they were in the field, Cain attacked his brother Abel and killed him.

Cain allowed his anger to develop into deep-seated hatred. When we allow anger to fester like that, it can lead to awful consequences.

Thankfully, John does not simply leave us with a negative example to warn us. John also gives us a positive example to pull us out of our own downward spirals. The positive example John gives us is Jesus Christ who laid down his life for us. Jesus laid down his life to pay for sin like Cain's, to pay for our sins, to pay for the sins of everyone: past, present and future.

Furthermore, by the power of Christ living in us through his Holy Spirit, we can follow Jesus' example. We can lay down our lives for our brothers and sisters. We can give of our material possessions to help those in need. We can love others, not just with words, but also in actions and in truth.

Fritz Ridenour tells the story of Boris Kornfeld who was a Russian medical doctor sentenced to a Communist slave labor camp for an unspecified political crime. Kornfeld's background was Jewish, but he had not practiced his religion for many years. In prison, a Christian led Kornfeld into a personal relationship with Jesus Christ.

Dr. Kornfeld began to take a stand against the hospital orderlies who would steal food from the patients; he also refused to remain silent when prison guards brutalized those prisoners under their charge and many prisoners died as a result.

Kornfeld became a marked man. He slept in his prison hospital office because he knew that if he slept on the prison ward itself someone might kill him.

At the same time that Kornfeld was taking a stand for justice, he also longed to tell someone about his newfound faith in Jesus Christ. One afternoon, as Dr. Kornfeld examined a young man who had received an operation to remove stomach cancer, Kornfeld began to share what a difference Jesus had made in his life. In fact, he spoke with this young patient all afternoon and into the night as the patient drifted in and out of a feverish sleep and painful waking moments. The young man could not quite believe what Kornfeld was telling him, but he was intrigued.

At last, the young patient fell asleep and slept through the night. When he awoke the next morning, a fellow patient told him that someone had attacked and killed Kornfeld in the night.

However, because of Kornfeld's witness, that young patient eventually became a Christian, survived the prison camp, and wrote of his experience in a number of books. That young patient was Alexander Solzhenitsyn.

Boris Kornfeld followed the loving example of Jesus Christ, and so can we, as Jesus' Spirit lives in us. Maybe we will not have the opportunity to follow Jesus' example by giving our lives in martyrdom, but we can give our lives away in little ways, every day, nonetheless.

Finally, in this passage, John not only talks about two attitudes and two examples, he talks about two destinations. The first destination John talks about is death. "Anyone who does not love remains in death." If we harbor hatred in our hearts, then we remain in death. Anger leads to hatred, if anger is not handled correctly, and hatred leads to death, unless we hand our hatred over to Jesus to deal with it. Hatred not only can lead to the physical death of those we hate, as in the story of Cain and Abel, but it can lead to our own death if we do not hand our hatred over to Jesus and allow him to extinguish it.

This is why it is so important to forgive when others hurt us. We need to forgive, not only for the positive result it can have on others, but also for the positive result it can have on us. If we do not forgive, bitterness will destroy us, it will swallow us up. The end result of hatred and bitterness eating away at us is death, not only physical death, but what is worse, spiritual death, separation from God who is the source of all light and life and love.

The alternative destination to spiritual death is, of course, life in all of its fullness. How can we know that we have passed from death to life? John says, "We know that we have passed from death to life, because we love each other."

Love is the key that unlocks the door to eternal life: God's love for us expressed in his Son Jesus, and our loving response to that love demonstrated in real life acts of love.

Think of it, every day not only are we heading to one of these final destinations ourselves, either life or death, but by our acts of love or hatred we are helping others to move to one of these destinies.

C. S. Lewis put it this way in his sermon entitled *The Weight of Glory*....

> It is a serious thing to live in a society of possible gods and goddesses, to remember that the dullest and most uninteresting person you can talk to may one day be a creature which, if you saw it now, you would be strongly tempted to worship, or else a horror and a corruption such as you now meet, if at all, only in a nightmare. All day long we are, in some degree, helping each other to one or other of these destinations. It is in the light of these overwhelming possibilities, it is with the awe and the circumspection proper to them, that we should conduct all our dealings with one another, all friendships, all loves, all play, all politics.

God's Love Letter

There are no ordinary people. You have never talked to a mere mortal. Nations, cultures, arts, civilizations—these are mortal, and their life is to ours as the life of a gnat. But it is immortals whom we joke with, work with, marry, snub, and exploit—immortal horrors or everlasting splendours.... Next to the Blessed Sacrament itself, your neighbour is the holiest object presented to your senses. If he is your Christian neighbour, he is holy in almost the same way, for in him also Christ *vere latitat*—the glorifier and the glorified, Glory Himself, is truly hidden.

Confidence Before God

Recently, I read a book that was a great help to me. The title was *Shame & Grace: Healing the Shame We Don't Deserve* by Lewis B. Smedes. Lew Smedes was, for many years, a professor at the School of Psychology at Fuller Theological Seminary in Pasadena, California. At the beginning of the book, Smedes shares this story about his mother....

> I was visiting with her at the hospital one afternoon. She was going to die in a few weeks, though only she knew it. The winter sun was setting, she was bone-tired—we had talked too long—her eyes closed now. Moist at the corners, and she heaved, "O Lewis, I'm so glad that the Lord forgives me all of my sins; I've been a great sinner, you know."
>
> Great sinner? As far back as I could remember, she was on her knees scrubbing people's kitchen floors most days, up to her neck in the frets of five fussing children every evening, and, when late night fell, there she was on her knees again, in her own kitchen this time, asking the Lord for strength to do it again for one more day. When did she have time and where did she get the energy to do any great sinning?
>
> What she was feeling about herself in those last weeks was what she had been feeling most of her life, that she was just not good enough, not a good enough mother, or a good enough Christian, or a good enough anything she could think of. But not being good enough felt to her the same as being very bad. And "great sinner" was the only way she could think of to describe the heaviness she felt.... My mother had a classic case of unhealthy shame. A lifelong affair with chronic not-good-enoughness. I learned my shame from her.
>
> It saddens me still that such a triumph of a woman should have to die feeling like a wretch. Her shame was totally out of touch with her reality. She did not deserve to be stuck with so much shame.

I believe that unhealthy shame is one of the problems that John addresses in the next section of his letter. He knows that some of the things he has said already in this letter may be producing in some of his readers this very unwanted and unnecessary shame, so he wants to nip it in the bud before it spreads. Let's read what John has to say on this very important topic from 1

God's Love Letter

John 3:19-24….

> This is how we know that we belong to the truth and how we set our hearts at rest in his presence: If our hearts condemn us, we know that God is greater than our hearts, and he knows everything. Dear friends, if our hearts do not condemn us, we have confidence before God and receive from him anything we ask, because we keep his commands and do what pleases him. And this is his command: to believe in the name of his Son, Jesus Christ, and to love one another as he commanded us. The one who keeps God's commands lives in him, and he in them. And this is how we know that he lives in us: We know it by the Spirit he gave us.

John tells us that the way to heal the shame we do not deserve is to realize that God is greater than our hearts. How does this knowledge heal our shame? Well, it is like this: all of us have a conscience. That, in essence, is what John is talking about here, except that he uses the word "heart" instead of conscience. The problem with our conscience is that it does not work correctly all the time. In some people, conscience is underactive. I imagine this has been true of many of the great tyrants down through history. Hitler had more than six million Jews killed in the gas chambers. If he ever felt guilt or shame over that horrendous evil, history has failed to record it. That is an extreme example of an underactive conscience.

On the other end of the spectrum is the case of many religious people. Many of us have overactive consciences. That is what John is talking about when he says: "if our hearts condemn us". Certainly there are many times when our hearts condemn us properly: when we lie, cheat, steal, are unfaithful to our spouse, fail to honor our parents, fail to put God first in our lives. When we feel guilty about such failures, John has already told us what we should do: we should confess our sins to God and receive his forgiveness through his Son Jesus Christ by the power of the Holy Spirit. When we do that, John tells us what happens: "If we confess our sins, he [God] is faithful and just and will forgive us our sins and purify us from all unrighteousness." (1 John 1:9)

However, sometimes we feel a vague sense of guilt, we feel shame, about thoughts, feelings, or actions about which we have no right to feel shame or guilt. What do we do then? We need to realize that God is greater than our hearts; God is greater than our consciences. When our conscience puts us on trial, God is the final court of appeal. We can ask God: "Is what I have been thinking, doing, or saying, really wrong?" How will God answer us? God may answer us in any number of ways: perhaps through some words in Scripture, maybe through the words of a trusted friend or counselor, but always through the work of the Holy Spirit. The bottom line is that when our hearts condemn us, we need to experience God's grace and God's love that is greater than our hearts.

Lew Smedes tells one man's story of encounter with God's grace that heals shame. The man's name was Racehoss Sample....

> Racehoss was Big Emma's boy. Big Emma was a smashing prostitute who made a living by providing gambling and bootleg liquor along with the sex she sold in a shack near a railroad stop in middle Texas. Racehoss got in Big Emma's way, and she resented him for it from the start. She beat him whenever she was drunk, which was a good deal of the time, and made him know that he was less than worthless.
>
> When he got to be eleven years old, Racehoss would not stand it anymore and took off; he ran away to nowhere special, riding the rails wherever they took him, riding them with bums and hoboes, and, along the way, becoming a creature of volcanic rage. The Second World War broke out, and the army found him but soon found out it could not tame him. He went AWOL every month or so, and each time he did, he got into a fight and was sent to jail for assault and battery. Finally, they sentenced him to thirty years in the Texas state penitentiary. Here he learned for sure that if you treat a person like an animal, he becomes one.
>
> The worst punishment they had for untamed prisoners was confinement in the tomb. The tomb was actually a four-by-eight-foot basement cell with no windows and two solid-steel plates for a door, a solid slab of concrete for a bed, a missing slab in the floor to pass for a toilet—the stench lingering on from occupant to occupant—and absolute darkness. This is where they stuck a prisoner who forgot to grovel low enough to suit his white boss, locked him in there for twenty-eight days, with one cup of water and one biscuit a day, and one meal of mush every six days to keep him alive.
>
> Racehoss spent a considerable amount of his time in the tomb. In the sixteenth year of his captivity, he contradicted one of the guards and was locked in again, but it was not the same this time. This time he was terrified as soon as they shoved him in. He heard a sound of rushing water nearby, and he knew for sure it was going to seep in and drown him. He went crazy.

Here is the rest of the story in Racehoss' own words....

> I ... ran around the walls. Then rolled on the floor like a ball.... I mauled myself, scratching and tearing at my body. Slumped, exhausted on the slab, I covered my face with both hands and cried out, "Help me

God's Love Letter

God!! Help meeeee!!"…

And then—

A ray of light between my fingers. Slowly uncovering my face, the whole cell was illuminated like a 40 watt bulb turned on. The soft light soothed me and I no longer was afraid. Engulfed by a presence, I felt it reassuring me. It comforted me…I breathed freely. I had never felt such well being, so good, in all my life. Safe. Loved.

The voice within talked through the pit of my belly. "You are not an animal. You are a human being." And "Don't you worry about a thing. But you must tell them about me."

After that, God was real. He found me in the abyss of the burning hell, uplifted and fed my hungry soul, and breathed new life into my nostrils.

The way that Racehoss Sample experienced God's grace may not be the way that you or I will experience it. That does not matter. God's grace comes to us in many ways and many forms. One thing is certain: when we experience God's grace, when we realize God is greater than our hearts and that God loves us, knowledge of that fact changes us. God's grace changed Racehoss Sample. He left prison and became the first ex-convict to ever work out of the governor's office, the first to serve as a probation officer, the first to serve on the State Bar of Texas as a division head. He received the Liberty Bell Award and became the Outstanding Crime Prevention Citizen of Texas in 1981. Racehoss received a full pardon and changed his name to Alfred Sample.

Once we begin to experience God's grace in such a way as to heal both our deserved and undeserved shame, John tells us there are several results that will follow from that experience…. The first result is that we will have confidence before God.

When we have experienced God's grace through Jesus Christ then we can approach God without fear, in total trust. The Greek word for confidence, παρρησιαν, means to speak with all boldness. The valued right of citizens in ancient Greece was free speech. Paul tells us we are citizens of heaven and adopted children of God. As such, we have the right of free speech before the throne of God. We can come before God with whatever is on our minds and in our hearts any hour of the day or night.

Paul Borthwick tells the following story.…

> I was traveling from Boston to Denver, and the departure area for my flight was buzzing with stern-looking men in dark suits talking into their lapels. I asked a flight attendant what was happening. She replied, "Just wait. You'll see."

Reflections on 1 John

> After we settled into our economy-class seats, two of the dark-suited men arrived in first class, followed by former President Gerald Ford. I sat a few rows away! I thought, I've never met a President before. I'll go introduce myself.
>
> But then I wondered, Why would he want to meet me? I didn't even vote for him!
>
> Then I remembered that during my years in seminary, I had met President Ford's son, Mike. So I marched toward first class. Before the Secret Service men could stop me, I spoke boldly: "President Ford, I just wanted to meet you. I know your son, Mike."
>
> We talked briefly, mostly about Mike. Mike's name gave me "authority" to approach the President.[30]

The same thing is true in our relationship with God. We can approach God with boldness because of our relationship with his Son Jesus who died for us. Boldness is the first result of having an experience of God's grace.

A second result of having an experience of God's grace is that we will receive from God what we ask of him.

How can this be? Does this mean we can ask God for a million dollars and receive it? The answer is yes and no. If we ask God for a million dollars in order to spend it on our own selfish concerns, then we are not going to receive it. Our receiving what we ask of God is dependent upon our obedience to God's commands, doing what pleases God. When our hearts are in tune with God's will then we will naturally ask God for those things that God wants to give us. In some cases that may mean: asking for and receiving a million dollars for God's kingdom purposes. In other situations, we may simply have to ask God for patience to endure and God will give us that patience. However, the main thing we need to see here is that we can ask God with boldness for whatever we need because of what Jesus has done for us on the cross.

John Newton, author of *Amazing Grace*, once said,

> Thou art coming to a King,
> large petitions with thee bring,
> for His grace and power are such
> that none can ever ask too much.

Steve DeNeff and Dave Drury tell the following story in their book, *Soul Shift*:

> One time, my dad wanted to congratulate me on something I had accomplished in the sixth grade. He took me to K-Mart and made a wide sweeping gesture with his hand toward the whole store from the entrance. He said, "To congratulate you, I'll buy you anything in this

whole store tonight." My eyes widened as I thought of the possibilities.

At the time, I didn't have a full grasp on how money worked or how much money Dad had. So I sort of limited things in my mind. I didn't even look at the huge stereo systems, expensive bikes, or anything that cost more than one hundred dollars. Instead, I chose a cassette tape case that was less than fifty dollars. I was content with just that case. It was more than I could afford myself, for sure, so I chose that one. It was nice. Only many years later did I find out from Dad that he had one thousand dollars cash in his pocket that night. What's more, he brought his checkbook just in case that wasn't enough. In my selection, I limited his blessing in my life.

Imagine how much God has in his pocket for you. You don't ask God for all the spiritual power you could because you forget that you are his child. Like me and my earthly father, you don't realize all he could do for you, in you, and through you.[31]

This leads to the question: what are the specific commands we need to obey in order to receive what we ask of God?

John gives a very simple answer to that question: "And this is his command: to believe in the name of his Son, Jesus Christ, and to love one another as he commanded us."

We need to believe and love. In the Greek language of this passage, the verb "believe" is in the aorist tense. This means John is thinking of belief in terms of a one time, past action. John is talking about when we first come to faith in Christ. However, the verb "love" is in the present tense, thus indicating a continuing action. Love is to be the constantly expressed action that demonstrates our faith in Jesus Christ. Love and faith go together.

In his book, *Sources of Strength*, President Jimmy Carter shared this lesson.

After a personal witnessing experience with Eloy Cruz, an admirable Cuban pastor who had surprising rapport with very poor immigrants from Puerto Rico, I asked him for the secret of his success. He was modest and embarrassed, but he finally said, "Senor Jimmy, we only need to have two loves in our lives. For God, and for the person who happens to be in front of us at any time." That simple yet profound theology has been a great help to me in understanding the Scriptures. In essence, the whole Bible is an explanation of those two loves.[32]

John tells us something similar. If we believe in God's Son Jesus Christ and love others, then we can ask God for whatever we need and God will give it to us; if we believe and love then we will enjoy great success in life.

John goes on to tell us that the ones who believe and love actually have God living in them and they live in God. In fact, we cannot believe in Jesus or love others without God's help, without God living in us.

You may rightly ask: how do we know that we have God living in us? We know because God has given us the Holy Spirit to assure us. The Holy Spirit is ultimately the one who gives us confidence before God the Father.

We end this chapter where we began, with the words of Lew Smedes, who so wonderfully describes the experience of God coming to live in us by the Holy Spirit, the experience of grace that heals our shame....

> The grace of God comes to us in our scrambled spiritual disorder, our mangled inner mess, and accepts us with all our unsorted clutter, accepts us with all our potential for doing real evil and all our fascinating flaws that make us such interesting people. He accepts us totally as the spiritual stew we are.
>
> We are accepted in our fantastic contradictions and our boring corruptions. Accepted with our roaring vices and our purring virtues. We are damaged masterpieces, stunted saints, there are ogres and angels in our basements that we can hardly tell apart and that we have not dared to face up to. For the whole shadowed self each one of us is, grace has one loving phrase: you are accepted. Accepted. Accepted. Accepted.
>
> Grace heals our shame, at the beginning, not by taking all our shame away and not by separating the sheep of undeserved shame from the goats of deserved shame but by removing the one thing all our shame makes us fear the most: rejection. Nothing that could make us unacceptable will keep God from accepting us.
>
> No one whose shame is healed by grace has any reason to suppose he or she will in this life ever be pure light. She may in the energy of grace become more of the true self she is meant to be. The inner shadows may get lighter. Some of her ogres may give way to her angels. However, she will never be so pure of heart that grace is not needed nor so poor of spirit that grace will not accept her.

Test the Spirits

In his book *The Gospel according to Starbucks*, Leonard Sweet tells the story of Ed Faubert. Faubert is what you call a "cupper"—in layman's terms, he is a coffee-taster. The state of New York has actually certified Faubert's perspicacious taste buds. So refined is Faubert's sense of taste for coffee that even while blindfolded, he can take one sip of coffee and tell you "not just that it is from Guatemala, but from what state it comes, at what altitude it was grown, and on what mountain."[33]

Just as there are many different types of coffee in the world and it requires an expert to determine where a particular coffee bean comes from, so also in the spiritual realm there are many different spirits and spiritual discernment is required to determine where each spirit comes from.

In this next section of his letter, John tells us how to discern where a particular spirit comes from, a very necessary skill in our world today. Let's look together at what he says in 1 John 4:1-6....

> Dear friends, do not believe every spirit, but test the spirits to see whether they are from God, because many false prophets have gone out into the world. This is how you can recognize the Spirit of God: Every spirit that acknowledges that Jesus Christ has come in the flesh is from God, but every spirit that does not acknowledge Jesus is not from God. This is the spirit of the antichrist, which you have heard is coming and even now is already in the world.
>
> You, dear children, are from God and have overcome them, because the one who is in you is greater than the one who is in the world. They are from the world and therefore speak from the viewpoint of the world, and the world listens to them. We are from God, and whoever knows God listens to us; but whoever is not from God does not listen to us. This is how we recognize the Spirit of truth and the spirit of falsehood.

The first important thing that John tells us here is: *do not believe every spirit*.

Imagine what would happen if we believed every spirit, every religious prophet in the world. We would never get anything done in life because we would first be turning this way, and then that.

Reflections on I John

Do you know how many different religions there are in the world today? Yahoo Answers on the Internet lists twenty-one different major religions. Adherents.com lists twenty-two major religions.

Do you know how many different Christian denominations there are? In 2011, the Pew Forum on Religion & Public Life estimated that there were 41,000 different Christian denominations worldwide.

Now consider how many different movements or denominations are within each of the other major religions of the world. Then, think about how many so-called prophets in the world today may not fit under the category of any major religion.

Clearly, there are many spirits, many prophets, speaking in the world today. If we were to believe every one of them then we would, literally, all turn into spiritual schizophrenics.

Thankfully, John gives us a remedy for the problem of spiritual schizophrenia. He says: "test the spirits to see whether they are from God."

Unlike the expert coffee taster who can tell you what mountain in Guatemala a particular coffee bean comes from, spiritual taste testing is not the preserve of a few experts. John addresses *all* believers in the church; he calls us all "dear friends", or "beloved". John tells us that all of us as Christians have the ability to do appropriate and accurate spiritual taste testing.

The Greek word that John uses, translated as "test," is δοκιμαζετε. This word was used in ancient times to refer to testing metals for genuineness. Thus, the idea behind this word is that of testing something with a view toward approval. The same word is used in Luke 14:19 about a man who is going to test some oxen.

This word suggests that the Christian should not test spiritual teachings in the world in such a way that he or she hopes to find fault. Rather, we should be on the lookout for what is good.

I know professing Christians who have a very hard time finding anything good to say about any of the Christian congregations in their area. There is no church that is good enough for them. Thus, they do not attend worship services anywhere. Instead, they run their own home Bible study group and they follow the teachings of a well-known radio preacher. I often wonder if they lived near the church of that radio preacher and attended his services on a regular basis if they would find fault with him as well.

God does not want us as believers in his Son Jesus Christ to be faultfinders. He wants us to look for the good in other Christians and even in other religions. C. S. Lewis once wrote,

> If you are a Christian you do not have to believe that all the other religions are simply wrong all through. If you are an atheist you do

> have to believe that the main point in all the religions of the whole world is simply one huge mistake. If you are a Christian, you are free to think that all these religions, even the queerest ones, contain at least some hint of the truth. When I was an atheist I had to try to persuade myself that most of the human race have always been wrong about the question that mattered to them most; when I became a Christian I was able to take a more liberal view. But, of course, being a Christian does mean thinking that where Christianity differs from other religions, Christianity is right and they are wrong. As in arithmetic—there is only one right answer to a sum, and all other answers are wrong: but some of the wrong answers are much nearer being right than others.[34]

Thus, as we test the spirits we should not be naïve. We should realize that many false prophets have gone out into the world. However, we should not be nitpicky or faultfinding when it comes to examining religious beliefs. We should approach our spiritual taste testing with an attitude of looking for what is good, for what we can approve.

Now, here is the big question: how can we recognize a spirit that comes from God? How can we recognize a message that God wants us to listen to and believe?

John says there is one simple question we need to ask: *does this spirit, or prophet, confess that Jesus Christ has come in the flesh?* Every spirit or prophet that confesses that Jesus has come in the flesh is from God. Every spirit or prophet that does not confess this truth is not from God, but rather is of the antichrist.

John is saying there are actually *two* essential things we need to look for in the teaching of every spirit or prophet. *First, does this spirit or prophet acknowledge that Jesus is the Christ, the Messiah?*

Let us unpack that question into several sub-questions: Does this spirit or prophet believe and teach that Jesus is our great prophet, priest and king? In other words, does this spirit or prophet confess that Jesus is the one we should listen to above every other prophet? Does this spirit or prophet acknowledge Jesus as our great high priest who sacrificed himself on the cross for our sins? Does this spirit or prophet bow to the kingship, the lordship, and the leadership of Jesus? That is what is wrapped up in the seemingly simple confession of Jesus as Messiah.

Secondly, does this spirit or prophet acknowledge that Jesus has come in the flesh? This is precisely what the Gnostics in John's day, and shortly thereafter, denied. According to the Gnostics, matter was completely evil. Therefore, the idea that God would take on human flesh was impossible, unthinkable.

Many years later, Augustine said that in the pagan philosophers he could find parallels for everything in the New Testament except for one saying: "The Word became flesh."

Reflections on I John

As John saw it, to deny the humanity of Jesus was to strike at the very root of the Christian faith.

William Barclay notes five consequences if we deny the humanity of Jesus. First, to deny the humanity of Jesus is to deny that Jesus can ever be our example. If Jesus was not a real human being, living under the same conditions as other human beings, then he cannot show us how to live.

Second, to deny Jesus' full humanity is to deny that Jesus can be our high priest who opens the way to God. The writer to the Hebrews says that the true high priest must be like us in all things, knowing our weaknesses and temptations (Hebrews 4:14-15). To lead human beings to God the high priest must be human, otherwise he will be pointing us down a road that is impossible for us to take.

Third, to deny the humanity of Jesus is to deny that he can, in any real sense, be our savior. To save humanity Jesus had to identify with humanity, and that is what Christians believe the Son of God did in the fullest sense.

Fourth, to deny the full humanity of Jesus is to deny the salvation of the body. Christianity is quite clear about the fact that salvation is for the entire human person. Jesus saves our bodies as well as our souls. If we deny Jesus' full humanity then we deny that our bodies can ever become the temples of the Holy Spirit.

Finally, to deny the humanity of Jesus is to deny that there can ever be any real union between God and human beings. If spirit is completely good and the body is completely evil, as the Gnostics claimed, then God and human beings can never meet. They might meet when humanity has gotten rid of the body. Human beings and God might meet in some rarefied, disembodied, spiritual experience. However, what Christianity teaches is that because of God taking on human flesh in Jesus there can be real communion here and now between God and human beings.

In his book *Unspeakable*, Os Guinness tells the story about a well-known Christian leader whose son died in a cycling accident. Although the leader was devastated, somehow he managed to suppress his grief, even preaching eloquently at his son's funeral. His display of hope in the midst of tragedy earned him the admiration of many.

However, a few weeks after the funeral, the man invited Guinness and a few friends to his home. According to Guinness, this man spoke and even screamed "not with the hope of a preacher but with the hurt of a father—pained and furious at God, dark and bilious in his blasphemy." In his agony, he blamed God for his son's death.

Rather than rebuke him, one of Guinness's friends gently reminded the enraged father about the story of Jesus at Lazarus' tomb. On three occasions in that story, Jesus expressed anger, and even furious indignation, in the presence of death. When Jesus came to earth, he became a human being just like us, feeling the abnormality of our suffering. In Jesus' humanity we see God's perspective on our pain: the beautiful world God created is now broken and in ruins. Jesus will heal this broken world and our broken lives, but first, he came to earth in order to identify with our anguish.

Guinness concludes that when we understand Jesus' humanity, it frees us to face the world's brokenness just as Jesus did. Like Jesus, we are "free to feel what it is human to feel: sorrow at what is heartbreaking, shock at what is shattering, and outrage at what is flagrantly out of joint.... To pretend otherwise is to be too pious by half, and harder on ourselves than Jesus himself was."[35]

How do we overcome the spirits in this world who would deny the full humanity of Jesus? We can overcome the false prophets of this world by the power of the one who lives inside us. For the one who is in us is greater than the one who is in the world.

Who is the one who is in us? John does not mention his name here, but he did at the end of chapter three: the Holy Spirit. The Holy Spirit of God is greater than every other spirit and can overcome the one who is in the world, the antichrist. In fact, the Holy Spirit will one day overcome every anti-messiah spirit. In Philippians 2:9-11 we read about Jesus...

> Therefore God exalted him to the highest place
> and gave him the name that is above every name,
> that at the name of Jesus every knee should bow,
> in heaven and on earth and under the earth,
> and every tongue confess that Jesus Christ is Lord,
> to the glory of God the Father.

I like what William Barclay says about this....

> We have seen again and again that it is characteristic of him [the author of 1 John] to see things in terms of black and white. His thinking does not deal in shades. On the one side there is the man whose source and origin is God and who can hear the truth; on the other side there is the man whose source and origin is the world and who is incapable of hearing the truth. There emerges a problem, which very likely John did not even think of. Are there people to whom all preaching is quite useless? Are there people whose defences can never be penetrated, whose deafness can never hear, and whose minds are for ever shut to the invitation and command of Jesus Christ?
>
> The answer must be that there are no limits to the grace of God and that there is such a person as the Holy Spirit. It is the lesson of life that

the love of God can break every barrier down. It is true that a man can resist; it is, maybe, true that a man can resist even to the end. But what is also true is that Christ is always knocking at the door of every heart, and it is possible for any man to hear the voice of Christ, even above the many voices of the world.

Therefore, in the end we must recognize that the ultimate spiritual battle in the world is not between us Christians and every other group that does not acknowledge Christ. The battle is between the Holy Spirit and every antichrist spirit. We have to let the Holy Spirit do battle and not become argumentative ourselves. We must simply trust that the Holy Spirit and the love of Christ are going to win in the end.

Pastor Victor Pentz provides the following illustration....

> There's a wonderful story by Isak Dinesen called *Babette's Feast*, about a strict, dour, fundamentalist community in Denmark. Babette works as a cook for two elderly sisters who have no idea that she once was a chef to nobility back in her native France. Babette's dream is to return to her beloved home city of Paris, so every year she buys a lottery ticket in hopes of winning enough money to return. And every night her austere employers demand that she cook the same dreary meal: boiled fish and potatoes, because, they say, Jesus commanded, "Take no thought of food and drink."
>
> One day the unbelievable happens: Babette wins the lottery! The prize is 10,000 francs, a small fortune. And because the anniversary of the founding of the community is approaching, Babette asks if she might prepare a French dinner with all the trimmings for the entire village.
>
> At first the townspeople refuse: "No, it would be sin to indulge in such rich food." But Babette begs them, and finally they relent, "As a favor to you, we will allow you to serve us this French dinner." But the people secretly vow not to enjoy the feast and instead to occupy their minds with spiritual things, believing God will not blame them for eating this sinful meal as long as they do not enjoy it.
>
> Babette begins her preparations. Caravans of exotic food arrive in the village, along with cages of quail and barrels of fine wine.
>
> Finally the big day comes, and the village gathers. The first course is an exquisite turtle soup. The diners force it down without enjoyment. But although they usually eat in silence, conversation begins to take off. Then comes the wine: Veuve Cliquot 1860, the finest vintage in France. And the atmosphere changes. Someone smiles. Someone else giggles. An arm comes up and drapes over a shoulder. Someone is heard to say,

"After all, did not the Lord Jesus say, love one another?" By the time the main entrée of quail arrives, those austere, pleasure-fearing people are giggling and laughing and slurping and guffawing and praising God for their many years together. This pack of Pharisees is transformed into a loving community through the gift of a meal. One of the two sisters goes into the kitchen to thank Babette, saying, "Oh, how we will miss you when you return to Paris!" And Babette replies, "I will not be returning to Paris, because I have no money. I spent it all on the feast."[36]

I wonder: which version of Christianity are we living out today? Are we like the strict, dour fundamentalists of Denmark refusing to enjoy God and the life with which he has blessed us, or are we like Babette? Does the very quality of our life invite the world to suffer through somber religion or to delight in a rich feast of joy?

Something tells me that the Babettes of this world are going to win in the end because there is something about Babette that is very like Jesus Christ.

Napoleon Bonaparte is reported to have said, "Alexander, Caesar, and Hannibal conquered the world but they had no friends.... Jesus founded his empire upon love, and at this hour millions would die for him.... He has won the hearts of men, a task a conqueror cannot do."[37]

Nineteenth century evangelist D. L. Moody once said, "If you can really make a man believe you love him, you have won him; and if I could only make people really believe that God loves them, what a rush we would see for the kingdom of God!"[38]

There is a very popular Christian book from author and speaker, Rob Bell. The title is simply, *Love Wins*. I believe that is a great summary of the Good News. Though there are many spirits abroad in the world, many prophets with many different messages, there is one prophet whose love and joy are going to win in the end.

God's Love & Ours

What is love, from a child's point of view? Here are some actual definitions of love given by children....

> "When my grandmother got arthritis, she couldn't bend over and paint her toenails anymore. So my grandfather does it for her all the time, even when his hands got arthritis too. That's love."
>
> "When someone loves you, the way they say your name is different. You know that your name is safe in their mouth."
>
> "Love is when someone hurts you, and you get so mad, but you don't yell at them because you know it would hurt their feelings."
>
> "Love is when my mommy makes coffee for my daddy and she takes a sip before giving it to him, to make sure the taste is okay."
>
> "Love is what's in the room with you at Christmas if you stop opening presents and listen."
>
> "Love is like a little old woman and a little old man who are still friends even after they know each other so well."
>
> "Love is when Mommy sees Daddy smelly and sweaty and still says he is handsomer than Robert Redford."
>
> "Love is when your puppy licks your face even after you left him alone all day."
>
> "You really shouldn't say 'I love you' unless you mean it. But if you mean it, you should say it a lot. People forget."[39]

In this next section of his letter, John gives us his definition of love. Let's read it together in 1 John 4:7-12....

> Dear friends, let us love one another, for love comes from God. Everyone who loves has been born of God and knows God. Whoever does not love does not know God, because God is love. This is how God showed his love among us: He sent his one and only Son into the world that we might live through him. This is love: not that we loved God, but that he loved us and sent his Son as an atoning sacrifice for our sins. Dear friends, since God so loved us, we also ought to love one

another. No one has ever seen God; but if we love one another, God lives in us and his love is made complete in us.

John begins this section of his letter with a simple command, "Dear friends let us love one another."

When we are young, we tend to think this command easy to fulfill. After all, it is easy to love a spouse, is it not? At least, it is easy until the honeymoon is over. When poverty comes our way, and we are arguing about finances, then love does not seem so easy. When sickness visits our home, and we have to care for a spouse who is no longer attractive, suddenly love is not easy at all.

Perhaps this is because we all start with a limited definition of love. The Greeks called it Eros, falling in love. However, when we fall out of love, then what do we do?

Think of another example. It seems easy to love a child, does it not? Who could not love a child, a baby, who is cute and cuddly? However, once we bring that child home from the hospital, it is not so easy to love, when the child keeps us up at night with constant crying. It is hard to love when we are bone-tired.

Again, we start with a limited definition of love. The Greeks called it "storge". Our English translation is: "affection". This is the type of love that develops naturally between a parent and a child. However, what do we do when that child turns into a rebellious teenager, who spends the night out drinking with friends and then smashes up the family car on the way home?

Here is yet another example: the love between friends. The Greeks called it "philia". Friends are great to have, are they not? At least, friends are great until they need us to help them move house, and they have a grand piano that has to be lugged from a third floor apartment to a new house across town.

Think about the love we ought to have for one another in the Church. It seems easy to love others when you first join a new congregation and you are getting to know new people for the first time. However, what do you do when someone hurts you through gossip or some other means? It is so easy to give up on the fellowship of the Church and want to run away and hide. We need a love for one another in Christ that is stronger than mere affection.

Eros, storge, and philia are all great in their own way. These feeling-based sorts of love get us started on the pathway, but they do not help us finish very well at all. We need an entirely different quality and strength of love to carry us through life and help us accomplish the nitty-gritty, dirty jobs of our everyday existence. For this we need agape, which John will tell us more about in a moment.

However, first we must ask a question: Why love one another at all?

John has a three-part answer. First, he says we should love one another because love comes from God. In other words, love is the way God created us to live. When we fail to live our lives in love, we are trying to cut the wood of life against the grain. Life just does not flow along very well without love.

Secondly, John says that everyone who loves has been born of God and knows God. In other words, if you want to be sure that you are God's child, not just by creation, but also by adoption, if you want to know God in a personal way, then you will get involved in the activity of loving. This is where you will discover God.

I think it is no accident that people who have left the Church in their college years often come back to Church when they become parents themselves. I believe the reason is because when we become parents, suddenly we realize that our personal resources in life are inadequate to carry on the job of love, even loving our own biological children. We suddenly recognize that we need help. Perhaps God can help us in our task of loving our children. Thus, we head back to Church to try to discover God, to find a love that will empower the engine of family life.

What does agape look like? Belden Lane tells this Jewish legend:

> Time before time, when the world was young, two brothers shared a field and a mill, each night dividing the grain they had ground together during the day. One brother lived alone; the other had a wife and a large family.
>
> Now, the single brother thought to himself one day, "It isn't fair that we divide the grain evenly. I have only myself to care for, but my brother has children to feed." So each night he secretly took some of his grain to his brother's granary to see that he was never without.
>
> But the married brother said to himself one day, "It isn't really fair that we divide the grain evenly, because I have children to provide for me in my old age, but my brother has no one. What will he do when he's old?" So every night he secretly took some of his grain to his brother's granary. As a result, both of them always found their supply of grain mysteriously replenished each morning.
>
> Then one night they met each other halfway between their two houses. They suddenly realized what had been happening and embraced each other in love. The legend is that God witnessed their meeting and proclaimed, "This is a holy place—a place of love—and here it is that my temple shall be built." So it was. The First Temple is said to have been constructed on that very site.[40]

Agape always thinks of the other and works for the other's good.

John is telling us something very simple, yet profound. As Mister Rogers once said, "Life is deep and simple, and what our society gives us is shallow and complicated."[41]

The deep yet simple thing John is telling us here is that: Wherever we see agape in action, there we are also seeing something of God. The converse is also true. Wherever we do not see agape, we are witnessing the absence of God. As John says, "Whoever does not love does not know God."

Why is this the case? John answers: because God is love. With this statement, we come to the very center, theologically, of John's letter. This statement is at the very core of what John wants to communicate to his readers.

Let us think about what this means. God is love. John is not simply talking about God's actions, though God's actions are loving. John is saying that love is the very essence of who God is. If we are looking for a definition of God, here is the best one: God is love.

As we talked about earlier in our study, Augustine once defined the Trinity in this way: God the Father is the lover, Jesus his Son is the beloved, and the Holy Spirit is the love between them. God is an energy, the energy of love itself, an energy that has been pulsating for all eternity and will indeed go on forever.

Les and Leslie Parrott, in their book entitled *Relationships*, offer this analogy:

> The sun only shines, just as God only loves. It is the nature of the sun to shine, to offer warmth and light. And it is the nature of God to love. We are free to get away from the sun—we can lock ourselves in a dark room—but we do not keep the sun from shining just because we put ourselves in a place where it cannot reach us.
>
> So it is with God's love. We can reject it, but God keeps on loving us. No matter what our choices, God still loves. And because God loves us, a relationship with God is possible.[42]

John knows that to simply say "God is love" is very abstract. Therefore, he brings matters down to earth. John says if you really want to know what love looks like, then look to Jesus of Nazareth. Jesus defines love. God demonstrated his love in Jesus. Supremely, God revealed his love for all people by offering himself as a sacrifice for sin in the form of Christ.

Once again, John uses the same word he used at the beginning of chapter two: hilasmos, sacrifice of atonement. The hilastrion was the mercy seat: that place on the Ark of the Covenant, between the wings of the cherubim, where the blood of the sacrifice would be placed on the Day of Atonement by the Jewish high priest. This was also the place where God appeared to his people.

Now, John is saying that Jesus is our place of atonement. Jesus is the place where we become one with God through his sacrifice on the cross. In that event, we see what love really is: agape, God's unconditional love for human beings. It is a love so great that our holy God offers himself completely on the cross for sinful humanity.

Time magazine carried an interesting story a number of years ago about former President George Herbert Walker Bush. It described a trip he took back to the South Pacific. During World War II, Bush had been a bomber pilot, and was shot down by Japanese antiaircraft fire. The article detailed Bush's return to the very spot where he was rescued from his downed aircraft.

During his return visit, Bush met with a Japanese gentleman who claimed to have witnessed Bush's rescue back in 1944. The man related that as he and others were watching the rescue take place, one of the man's friends remarked, "Surely America will win the war if they care so much for the life of one pilot."[43]

God loved you so much that when you were down, when you were stranded and in need of rescue, he became a human being and sacrificed his life so you could be retrieved. God would have done this for you if you had been the only person in need of rescue. Such great love surely will win in the end.

In his book *The Prodigal God*, Tim Keller uses the following story to illustrate how experiencing God's love can transform our lives:

> The acclaimed foreign film *Three Seasons* is a series of vignettes about life in postwar Vietnam. One of the stories is about Hai, a cyclo driver (a bicycle rickshaw), and Lan, a beautiful prostitute. Both have deep, unfulfilled desires. Hai is in love with Lan.... Lan lives in grinding poverty and longs to live in the beautiful world where she works, but in which she never spends the night. She hopes that the money she makes by prostitution will be her means of escape, but instead the work brutalizes and enslaves her.
>
> Then Hai enters a cyclo race and wins the top prize. With the money, he brings Lan to the hotel. He pays for the night and pays her fee. Then, to everyone's shock, he tells her he just wants to watch her fall asleep. Instead of using his power and wealth to have sex with her, he spends it to purchase a place for her for one night in a normal world, to fulfill her desire to belong. Lan finds such grace deeply troubling at first, thinking that Han has done this to control her. When it becomes apparent that he is using his power to serve rather than use her, it begins to transform her, making it impossible to return to a life of prostitution.

Keller notes that in a similar way God's unconditional love demonstrated in the sacrifice of his Son can transform us when we simply receive it. Keller asks: "Why wouldn't you want to offer yourself to someone like this? Selfless love destroys mistrust in our hearts toward God."[44]

What should our response be to such a love? John says, since God so loved us, we also ought to love one another. This brings us right back to where

God's Love Letter

we started.

John reminds us that no one has ever seen God. John is probably thinking of the story of Moses who asked to see God and God allowed Moses to see only his backside. Sinful human beings cannot handle a face-to-face encounter with a holy God.

However, John says that when we love one another, God actually lives in us and his love is made complete in us. Amazing! When we love one another, we have the privilege of thereby showing God to the world.

John Trent writes,

> When I led a Young Life group, I did my best to round up kids who really needed to hear the gospel when we went to summer camp. Mark was one of those kids.
>
> Bob Mitchell, the main speaker that week, called most of the shots—including when meals would be served. So "Mitch" was always talking with the cook.
>
> The cook loved her work, but it was exhausting. She always looked tired. Whenever she talked to Mitch, he got up and gave her his chair—and a moment's rest—while they discussed meal plans. Nobody noticed Mitch doing this ... except Mark.
>
> Mark hadn't come to hear about Jesus. But when he saw Jesus' love lived out in that simple act of kindness by the camp speaker, he began to listen to his talks. Later that week, Mark asked Jesus to be his Savior.
>
> It wasn't because of the messages, Mark said, but because of the love he saw in Mitch.
>
> "If that's what it means to be a Christian," Mark said, "I want to be one."[45]

I wonder: who is there in your life, or in mine, to whom we might "give up our chair" this week? Doing so might just reveal the love of God to a watching world.

Blessed Assurance

After the economic downturn that began in 2008, Daniel Gilbert, a psychology professor at Harvard, stated that the Gallup-Healthways Well-Being Index showed "that Americans are smiling less and worrying more than they were a year ago, that happiness is down and sadness is up, that we are getting less sleep and smoking more cigarettes, that depression is on the rise."

He stated that the real problem is not financial—not having enough money, but something else: uncertainty. People do not know what is going to happen. Will I have a job next week? What is ahead in the future for me? Professor Gilbert pointed to a Dutch experiment where some subjects were told they would be intensely shocked 20 times. The researchers told a second group that they would receive three strong shocks and seventeen mild ones, but they would not know when the intense shocks would come. The result was that subjects in the second group sweated more and experienced faster heart rates. Uncertainty caused their discomfort, because they did not know when the shocks would come next.

Daniel Gilbert summarized, "An uncertain future leaves us stranded in an unhappy present with nothing to do but wait.... Our national gloom is real enough, but it isn't a matter of insufficient funds. It's a matter of insufficient certainty."[46]

What is true in the economic realm is also true in the spiritual realm: uncertainty makes us nervous. The good news is that God does not want us to live with spiritual uncertainty. Rather, he promises us blessed assurance. The question is: how do we access that assurance? That is the question John addresses in 1 John 4:13-21....

> This is how we know that we live in him and he in us: He has given us of his Spirit. And we have seen and testify that the Father has sent his Son to be the Savior of the world. If anyone acknowledges that Jesus is the Son of God, God lives in them and they in God. And so we know and rely on the love God has for us.
>
> God is love. Whoever lives in love lives in God, and God in them. This is how love is made complete among us so that we will have confidence on the day of judgment: In this world we are like Jesus. There is no fear

> in love. But perfect love drives out fear, because fear has to do with punishment. The one who fears is not made perfect in love.
>
> We love because he first loved us. Whoever claims to love God yet hates a brother or sister is a liar. For whoever does not love their brother and sister, whom they have seen, cannot love God, whom they have not seen. And he has given us this command: Anyone who loves God must also love their brother and sister.

The all-important question that John seeks to answer here is: How can we know that God lives in us? John gives us a five-part answer to that question.

First, we can know that God lives in us because: We have received God's Spirit.

Here John is reiterating the same point he made in 1 John 3:24. However, here he says that God has given us *of* his Spirit. Does this mean that it is possible to receive only part of God's Spirit? I believe the answer from the rest of the New Testament is a clear "no". It is impossible for us to have only part of the Spirit, but it is very possible that the Spirit has only part of us.

Let me explain....

The New Testament is quite clear that we receive the Holy Spirit when we first believe in Jesus. In Acts 2:38-39 we read what Peter said to the crowd who heard him preach on the day of Pentecost....

> Repent and be baptized, every one of you, in the name of Jesus Christ for the forgiveness of your sins. And you will receive the gift of the Holy Spirit. The promise is for you and your children and for all who are far off—for all whom the Lord our God will call.

Paul also makes it clear that without the Holy Spirit, we do not belong to Jesus. In Romans 8:9 he says,

> You, however, are not in the realm of the flesh but are in the realm of the Spirit, if indeed the Spirit of God lives in you. And if anyone does not have the Spirit of Christ, they do not belong to Christ.

Thus, we receive the Holy Spirit when we believe, and without the Holy Spirit, we cannot believe or belong to Christ at all. However, once we have the Spirit it is possible to limit the work of the Holy Spirit in our lives. Thus, Paul urges us:

> And do not grieve the Holy Spirit of God, with whom you were sealed for the day of redemption.

It is not possible to grieve an inanimate object, but because we have a personal relationship with God through the Holy Spirit living in our lives it *is* possible to grieve him, by our sin, by our neglect of the means of grace, by trying to live on our own power instead of his.

The alternative to grieving the Holy Spirit is to be filled with the Spirit. In Ephesians 5:18 Paul says, "Do not get drunk on wine, which leads to debauchery. Instead, be filled with the Spirit." This verse suggests that to be filled with the Holy Spirit is to come under his full control, just as when we drink too much alcohol we come under its control. God wants us to "drive under the influence" … but not of alcohol, rather of the Holy Spirit.

"But how do we know that we have the Holy Spirit in our lives when we cannot see him?"

That is a good question. Though we cannot see the Holy Spirit, we can see the fruit he produces. Paul tells us that the fruit of the spirit is: "love, joy, peace, patience, kindness, goodness, faithfulness, gentleness and self-control." (Galatians 5:22-23) The fruit of the spirit is one fruit with many aspects to it. The important thing is that when we see these qualities in our lives, we can be sure that they have been produced by the presence of the Holy Spirit, and because we have the Holy Spirit, we can be sure that we are living in God and he in us.

Lee Eclov tells this story....

> On the afternoon of May 2, 1990, I heard holy things. I was visiting Larry Hildreth, a father and husband from our church in Pennsylvania. He was in his thirties, but he was near death from cancer. I was at his home to serve him Communion, because he was too weak to come to church.
>
> Larry was a deeply thoughtful man, and as he spoke that day, slow and deliberately, I realized I was hearing extraordinary things. I started scribbling them down on the margins of a bulletin in my Bible.
>
> "Even if I have a short time to live," Larry said, "God has given me a great hope. Sometimes life throws us some tremendous curves, but death has lost its sting."
>
> In his struggle with cancer, it was clear that Larry had learned a lot about weakness. "At the point in my life when I'm the weakest," he said, "I'm the strongest I've ever been."
>
> We started talking about his funeral, which as it turned out, would be exactly one month later. He told me he wanted lots of singing. (I remember how in church Larry would put his head back and sing with such unabashed gusto.) He said, "The only thing I want people to think on that day is joy." As he said this, he raised his hands to offer a slow, triumphant clap. "When I pass into his kingdom, I envision this spectacular light—this spectacular feeling of being able to let go," he said. "I've felt a lot of grief for my children, my wife, my family, myself.

But I've had to get over that. And once you get past that, you know that God is there, [and there's] that spirit of joyfulness. It's going to be a happy day for me. No grief for me."

That is the kind of assurance that only the Holy Spirit can give us.

Secondly, John says we can be sure that God is living in us because: We have the testimony of the apostles. John writes, "And we have seen and testify that the Father has sent his Son to be the Savior of the world."

The presence of the Holy Spirit in our lives is a subjective source of assurance. However, the work of the Spirit is also tied to an objective source: the testimony of the apostles. Those who knew Jesus, who heard him speak and witnessed his miracles, told others what they had seen and heard and experienced, and within twenty years these stories began to be written down. This is what Jesus himself promised would happen:

> When the Advocate comes, whom I will send to you from the Father—the Spirit of truth who goes out from the Father—he will testify about me. And you also must testify, for you have been with me from the beginning. (John 15: 26-27)

In the New Testament, we have reliable testimony to Jesus from the first generation of his followers. As it says in 2 Peter 1:16….

> For we did not follow cleverly devised stories when we told you about the coming of our Lord Jesus Christ in power, but we were eyewitnesses of his majesty. He received honor and glory from God the Father when the voice came to him from the Majestic Glory, saying, "This is my Son, whom I love; with him I am well pleased." We ourselves heard this voice that came from heaven when we were with him on the sacred mountain.

If we want to gain assurance of our salvation, there is no better way than to prayerfully read the New Testament, asking the Holy Spirit to speak to us through it and give us the assurance for which we so long. However, rather than utilize this proven method, some people opt for shakier deals.

Peter Kouba ran a website called Heaven's Registry. For $20, Kouba offered: "guaranteed admission into heaven." Although police considered this a scam, detective Mark Johnson admitted: "It would be pretty tough to prove he's wrong."

The certificate was also available for "cherished pets" at a cost of $15.

Commenting on the report, pastor Alan Andrus said, "Our calling is to teach and to preach what's in the Bible. I guess there'll always be people who take advantage of people and use religion to do it."

The Heaven's Registry website warned that only God knows which faults will keep us out of heaven: "picking a flower in the park, eating a grape at the market without paying for it, breaking the law by speeding or going through a stop sign, using the Lord's name in vain, adultery and many more." After raising the specter of uncertainty, the website promised that with this 100% guaranteed heavenly admission certificate, there is now "no need for confessions or penance."[47]

Guess what? I checked and the web site is no longer in existence, as far as I could tell. Some assurance, is it not? How much better to go to God's Word in Scripture and ask the Holy Spirit for the assurance God promises to give.

A third way John tells us that we can receive assurance, a way spoken about in Scripture, is through acknowledging Jesus as the Son of God.

John writes, "If anyone acknowledges that Jesus is the Son of God, God lives in them and they in God."

Paul says something similar in Romans 10:9....

> If you declare with your mouth, "Jesus is Lord," and believe in your heart that God raised him from the dead, you will be saved.

Great peace of mind comes through publicly owning Jesus as Lord and Savior. I remember the tremendous peace I felt, and still feel, because I publicly declared my allegiance to Christ in a church service when I was thirteen years old. Confession of faith in Christ is something we do every Sunday as we recite The Apostles' Creed. Of course, making a confession of faith in Christ in church is not the only way we can acknowledge Jesus as the Son of God. This is something we can do in our everyday lives.

The animated story, *A Charlie Brown Christmas,* airs on one of the major television networks every year. The two producers who worked closely with Charlie Brown creator Charles Schultz remembered, in an interview, their desperate efforts to convince a network to show the special originally. All the major networks were hesitant. Finally, one agreed, and the great cartoonist got to work.

A memorable and moving part of *A Charlie Brown Christmas* occurs when the cartoon character Linus strolls to center stage and reads the biblical account of the birth of Christ. The two producers working with Schultz cautioned him about putting something like that in the special, because they were convinced it would not go over well. Charles Schultz faced both of the producers and said, "If not us, then who's going to do it?"[48]

That is a great question we probably all need to ask ourselves. We may not have the opportunity to acknowledge Jesus as the Son of God through a nationally syndicated television program, but we each have opportunities to confess Christ in our everyday lives. Furthermore, every time we do acknowledge Jesus, such action will fill us afresh with assurance of our own salvation. I have found that every time I tell someone else about the love of Jesus, I am strengthened in my own faith.

A fourth way that John says we can receive assurance that God is living in us and we in him is through an experience of God's love.

Our experience of God's love can be a growing thing in our lives. John says that we know and rely on the love God has for us. The more we put ourselves in situations where we must rely on God, where we must trust him to deliver us, the more we will experience his love.

God's love seeks completion in us. How does that happen? God's love is made complete through our becoming more like God's Son Jesus. That is a process. John says we are like Jesus in the world. Jesus was and is fully human. However, Jesus was and is fully divine as well. As God, Jesus can help us to become the perfect human beings he created us and redeemed us to be.

Jesus had no fear in relationship to his heavenly father. He trusted God completely as Abba. As Jesus lives in us by his Spirit, he can help remove any residual fear in our relationship with God. So long as we are afraid of God, of what he may do to us, such fear reveals that we have not fully experienced his love. God's love for us is total, perfect, unending, and unlimited. Therefore, we have nothing to fear from God, only wonderful things to look forward to receiving from his hand. The best is yet to be!

Skye Jethani relates a story about holding a series of meetings with college-aged students. The topics ranged across the spectrum—various church doctrines, hell, dating—but each conversation had three rules: be honest, be gracious, and be present. On one night, the students wanted to discuss habitual sins. Although they struggled with a variety of sinful behaviors, they all agreed on one thing: God was extremely disappointed with them. One student said, "My parents were students at a Christian college in the early '90s when a revival broke out…. They were on fire for God. And here I am consumed by sin day after day." Often through tears, many other students shared similar stories about how they believed God must be disappointed with them.

After listening to their stories, Jethani asked, "How many of you were raised in a Christian home?" They all raised their hands. "How many of you grew up in a Bible-centered church?" All hands stayed up. Shaking his head in disbelief, Jethani said, "You've all spent eighteen or twenty years in the church. You've been taught the Bible from the time you could crawl, and you attend Christian colleges, but not one of you gave the right answer. Not one of you said that in the midst of your sin God still loves you."

Jethani concluded: "I did not blame the students for their failure. Somewhere in their spiritual formation they were taught, either explicitly or implicitly, that what mattered was not God's love for them, but how much they could accomplish for him."[49]

Reflections on I John

Many of us have a similar mistaken notion about God. We think God is mad *at* us, when really he is mad *about* us. God loves you more than you could ever imagine.

The final way John tells us we can receive assurance that God is living in us and we in God is through loving our brothers and sisters in Christ.

When we truly experience the love of God then we will naturally overflow that love to others, not just to our fellow Christians, but also to everyone. "We love because he first loved us."

The story is told of two Christian co-workers who had a difficult time loving their non-Christian boss because he was often mean to them. Finally, the two Christians decided to get together during their lunch hour and pray for their boss, whom they knew was going to be away from his office during that time. They decided to pray for their boss in the setting of his private office, to which they had access as his assistants. Thus, during their lunch hour, they stood praying for their boss in his office and they decided to add a physical gesture to their prayer that would aid them in visualizing exactly what God wanted for their relationship with their employer. As they prayed, these two Christians each held up one hand toward heaven, visualizing the reception of God's love into their lives. Then with their other hand they gestured toward the door of their boss' office, thus indicating the love of God they desired to flow through them to their employer.

As they were praying in this dramatic way, suddenly their boss returned from lunch and asked them what they were doing. They explained that they were praying for their boss, for the love of God to fill his life.

I do not know how that man responded to the prayers of these two Christians, but the way these two people stood in prayer before God illustrates how we each need to walk through life. We need to go through every day with one hand stretched out to God to receive God's love and our other hand stretched out to our neighbor to share God's love with him or her. As we go through our days living out that posture, I believe we will receive great assurance that, indeed, God is living in us and we in God.

Faith & Its Effects

Author and Presbyterian pastor Eugene Peterson has written,

> What is hazardous in my life is my work as a Christian. Every day I put faith on the line. I have never seen God. In a world where nearly everything can be weighed, explained, quantified, subjected to psychological analysis and scientific control I persist in making the center of my life a God whom no eye hath seen, nor ear heard, whose will no one can probe. That's a risk.[50]

In 1 John 5:1-5 we learn more about the risk of faith, its nature and its effects….

> Everyone who believes that Jesus is the Christ is born of God, and everyone who loves the father loves his child as well. This is how we know that we love the children of God: by loving God and carrying out his commands. In fact, this is love for God: to keep his commands. And his commands are not burdensome, for everyone born of God overcomes the world. This is the victory that has overcome the world, even our faith. Who is it that overcomes the world? Only the one who believes that Jesus is the Son of God.

The first thing John tells us here is something about the nature of faith.

There is a phrase I often hear as a pastor. When someone faces a tragedy of some sort, the loss of a loved one, or a job layoff, or the trials and tribulations of dealing with a son or daughter wandering from God, people will say to that person dealing with tragedy: "Thank God for your faith." People make this statement thinking that there is some magic in faith itself, thinking that it does not matter what one's faith is in; all that matters is faith. However, such is not the case.

Faith is like a straw through which I suck the contents of a chocolate shake into my mouth. Can you imagine someone purchasing a shake at Dairy Queen, setting aside the shake, and being content simply licking the straw? No, we use the straw to get the delicious ice cream into our mouths where we can roll it over our tongues in total delight.

Faith is like that. It is simply a straw, a conduit, through which we receive something far more important. What matters is not so much faith itself, but faith's object.

According to John, the proper object of our faith is Jesus Christ. John tells us that everyone who believes that Jesus is the Christ, the Messiah, that person has had something miraculous happen to them. They have been born of God. Faith and spiritual rebirth are inseparably intertwined.

John is, of course, recalling once again the words of Jesus in the third chapter of The Gospel of John, "Very truly I tell you, no one can enter the kingdom of God unless they are born of water and the Spirit."

Paul says something similar in 1 Corinthians 12:3. He writes, "No one can say, 'Jesus is Lord,' except by the Holy Spirit."

Without spiritual rebirth we cannot see the kingdom of God. Without the Holy Spirit in our lives we cannot truly confess Jesus as Lord, Jesus as Master and Commander. Therefore, when we confess Jesus as Messiah, it is a sign that we have already been born of God. The key thing is not faith itself, but the One in whom our faith is placed.

Pastor Phil LeMaster tells the following story....

> It was nearing Christmas, and I received a phone call from a man who needed to talk to a counselor. I met him at my church office, where he told me his tale of woe. A decade earlier, he killed his wife in a fit of anger, was convicted of manslaughter, and spent several years in prison. He and his wife had a daughter who was in the custody of his in-laws. He had not seen her since the crime, and now, as Christmas neared, his heart ached. Tears streaming down his face, he lamented, "I could pass her on the streets of this city and not even know who she was."
>
> What I remember most about our counseling session, however, was what he said when he first walked into my office. Dramatically raising his arms he said, "Now, preacher, let's just leave Jesus out of this, okay?"
>
> As he sadly went his way that day, I thought to myself, That's the whole problem. You've left Jesus out.[51]

When we leave Jesus out of the equation, faith is just an empty straw.

We are probably all familiar with the blind hymn-writer Fanny Crosby. Instead of wallowing in self-pity because of her blindness, she trusted in Jesus Christ and wrote the hymns we still sing, like *To God Be the Glory* and *Blessed Assurance.*

When Fanny Crosby was old, somebody told her that, if she had been born in that day, an operation could have restored her sight. Instead of being bitter, she said, "I don't know that I would change anything. Do you know that the first thing I'm ever going to see is the face of Jesus?"[52]

Now there is someone who knew where her faith resided! Fanny Crosby's life was changed, and her life continues to positively impact the lives of others, not simply because she was a woman of faith, but because she placed her faith in Jesus as Messiah.

The second major point John makes in this passage is about the effects of faith.

If faith is a sign of spiritual rebirth, and I believe it is, then the effects of faith that John articulates are further signs of the new relationship that the Christian has with God. John points out three effects of faith, or three ways that faith is demonstrated in the life of the Christian.

However, before we look into each of these effects of faith, it is important to note that sometimes it is hard for us to see these effects in our own lives. Often these effects are more evident to others than they are to us. In fact, I surmise that some of us will not fully recognize these effects in our lives until we reach heaven.

The story is told about a particular woman who loved plants in general and flowers in particular. She planted a rare vine against a stone wall near the back of her yard. She nurtured the vine, and it grew well. The plant grew to be quite vigorous and beautiful. However, the woman never saw the blossoms that the vine was supposed to produce. Thus, she was very disappointed.

One day this woman stood looking at her vine with its beautiful foliage but no blossoms. Her neighbor called across the wall, asking her to come over to his yard. The woman went over to the other yard. The neighbor said, "Thank you for planting that vine. Look at these beautiful blossoms."

What had happened was this: the vine had crept through the stone wall, and the blossoms were on the other side. The woman who planted the vine simply had not seen them yet.

That is often the way of it when it comes to the effects of faith. Others often see those signs of faith in us before we do. Furthermore, sometimes we will not see the effects of faith until we "go over to the other side," until we reach heaven.[53]

What are the effects of faith that John articulates in this passage? The first is love, love for God and love for God's children. John says, "Everyone who loves the father loves his child as well."

John never tires of reminding us of what Jesus called the two great commandments: to love God with all our hearts, all our minds, and all our souls, and with all our strength, and to love our neighbors as ourselves. In a sense, this is really a three-part commandment. If we love God then we will love God's children, and each one of us are God's children. Therefore, we need to love ourselves, because as the saying goes: "God don't make no junk." When we truly receive God's love, and are therefore able to love ourselves more effectively, then we can go on to reflect that love back to God and outward to others.

Reflections on 1 John

Pastor Mike Breaux tells the following story of when his daughter Jodie answered God's call to go into missions work:

> During her junior year of high school, Jodie struggled to find a faith of her own. She wanted to know in her heart that all of what she'd been taught to believe was true and that Jesus Christ was real. Honestly, she was headed down a dark road. But God pursued her down that road. She eventually found a faith of her own, and when she graduated from high school, she said, "I don't think God wants me to go to college right now. I want to take a year to go to Haiti, and I want to serve people in a medical mission down there."
>
> I said, "Are you sure you want to do this? Jodie, it's 3,000 miles away from home. It's AIDS-infested and the poorest country in the western hemisphere. And do you know it's controlled by the voodoo religion?"
>
> "I know all that," she said. "But I feel like God wants me to go and help those people."
>
> I said, "Okay. If that's what you want to do, we'll make it happen."
>
> One of the hardest days of my life was putting my little girl on an airplane and watching it lift off, not knowing whether I'd ever communicate with her again.
>
> One night I got an e-mail from Jodie. She wrote: "Dad, tonight has been the most remarkable night of my life. I got called out to this hut to deliver a baby. Dad, I've only delivered one, and that was with somebody. I'd never done this by myself, but I was the only one around. They called me, and I get to this hut, and there's this naked, screaming lady on the dirt floor. I got a flashlight, and I'm thinking, Here I am, 18-years-old, and I'm in a hut in a third-world country with a naked, screaming, pregnant lady. I have a flashlight, and I don't know what I'm doing—but I'm here. To make matters worse, this lady from the voodoo religion walked into the hut, dressed in her red and blue voodoo garb, and began to chant some voodoo incantation in Creole. She put some kind of oil on the lady's head, and when she started to walk away from me and the woman, she stopped at the woman's belly, put some other kind of salve there, and walked the opposite direction—all while chanting this Creole spell. I didn't know what to do. She stood at the head of this woman and stared a hole through me. When I was getting ready to deliver this baby, I just looked back at her, and I started singing. I knew she didn't understand English, but I just started singing: 'Our God is an awesome God, he reigns from heaven above, with wisdom, power, and love, our God is an awesome God.'"

Jodie said that the voodoo lady became completely unglued. She grabbed all of her stuff and ran out of the hut. Jodie wrote, "That night I knew that that baby was going to be born with the blessing of God and not the curse of Satan."

As I read Jodie's e-mail, my fatherly side thought, You get on a plane tomorrow! What are you doing in a hut with a voodoo woman in the first place? But then my heart beat so fast for her as her brother in Christ. I thought, Way to go, Jodie! Way to make a difference with your life! Way to stop floating around accidental-like! Way to put your life in the hands of the destiny-maker! Way to make a splash! Who knows who that little baby she delivered that night is going to grow up to touch and who that person is going to touch—all because of one courageous girl who said, "Okay, God, I want to put my life in your hands; I want to make a difference."

In Mark 8:35 Jesus said: If you insist on saving your life—[if you insist on the comfort of playing it safe]—you're going to lose your opportunity for life! Only those who give away their lives for my sake and for the sake of the Good News will ever know what it really means to really, really live.[54]

    I believe Jodie is an example of someone who has experienced the love of God. Thus, she has been enabled to love herself and thereby reflect that same love back to God and outward to others. Love is the first effect of faith that John articulates.

    The second effect of faith goes right along with the first. It is obedience.

    How do we know that we are really showing love to others? John says we can be sure that we are loving God's children if we love God first and carry out God's commands. In fact, John says, to keep God's commands is to love God.

    This is true in every parent-child relationship. If I ask one of my sons to do something for me, and they refuse to do it, that refusal shows that my son really does not love or respect me. Now, I am human, and therefore fallible and sinful. Sometimes I may ask my sons to do something that is wrong, or I may ask them out of the wrong motive. However, God is good all the time. God never asks us to do anything wrong, nor does he ever ask us to do something for him out of the wrong motive. God's motives are always perfect and good. Thus, there is never any reason why we should not obey God, and when we do obey God that obedience demonstrates our love for God. Our love for God should be demonstrated in concrete acts.

    Furthermore, John points out that God's commands are not burdensome. If we are God's children then we are going to want to obey God. Obeying God is what we were created to do.

Reflections on I John

Sometimes we get the mistaken notion that if we surrender ourselves completely to God then God will send us somewhere we do not want to go, or make us do something we do not want to do. However, such is not the case. As the Westminster Shorter Catechism states, our chief end is to glorify God and to enjoy God forever. That is what we were created to do. In fact, we most glorify God when we are enjoying God. The two go together. Glorifying and enjoying God are not laborious tasks.

As Frederick Buechner has said, "The place God calls you to is the place where your deep gladness and the world's deep hunger meet."[55]

The third effect of faith that John points out in this passage is: victory. John says,

> Everyone born of God overcomes the world. This is the victory that has overcome the world, even our faith. Who is it that overcomes the world? Only the one who believes that Jesus is the Son of God.

John is certainly echoing the words of Jesus in John 16:33, "I have told you these things, so that in me you may have peace. In this world you will have trouble. But take heart! I have overcome the world."

Jesus promises us at least four things in life: peace, power, purpose, and trouble! To follow Jesus is to go against the grain of the world; to follow him means going against the flow. Thus, there will be opposition for the true Christian. There will be some form of persecution. Jesus experienced trouble; therefore, Jesus' followers can count on experiencing problems too.

However, the good news is that Jesus overcame all the troubles of this world through his death and resurrection. Therefore, as we put our trust in Jesus, we too will overcome. By the straw of faith, we can suck Jesus' own victory into ourselves.

Lyn Cryderman shared the following Korean faith story in *Christianity Today* a number of years ago....

> Kim Duk-Soo will never forget November 20, 1950. That was the day Communist troops found him hiding with his father in a root cellar.
>
> Kim, now the administrator of Presbyterian Hospital in Taegu, has difficulty telling his story. He is not alone. Hundreds of thousands of Christians made up the human wave escaping the North for the free South. And each has a similar story of deliverance from a regime opposed to religion.
>
> "When we heard the soldiers coming, I was sure we would be killed," says Kim, his eyes filling with tears. "My Daddy told me we could not tell a lie to save our lives."
>
> Kim's father had pastored the same church for 42 years. He had helped

his wife hide their children by covering them with rice bags and dirt. But after two days of hiding, Kim uncovered himself. Just then, Communist troops approached the house. Kim and his father ran to the back yard and hid in the root cellar.

"I told God I would serve him all my life if I got out of the root cellar alive."

The soldiers found Kim and his father and took them off to a makeshift prison. They were to be executed the next morning. That evening, a captain approached Kim. "Are you a Christian?" he asked. For a fleeting moment, life for a lie seemed the only logical way to go. But the young boy remembered his father's instruction.

"I am a Christian," Kim said.

The captain drew closer, and whispered, "I am a Christian too. I used to be a Sunday school teacher before the war. You must escape tonight. I will help you." Kim fled that night, having to leave his father under heavy guard awaiting his eventual death.

The young Kim reached an American army base, and while "hanging around" there discovered an organ and began teaching himself to play. An American he remembers only as Captain Shoemaker learned of his musical interests and ordered a spinet from the States. For the next ten years, Kim played that organ for chapel services at the base.

It is Mother's Day at First Presbyterian in Taegu. "A Mighty Fortress" reverberates from 2,000 Korean voices. As he has done for 30 years, Kim plays the organ. "I should have been killed after the Communists found me, but God sent that Christian guard to help me escape. When I play the organ at church. I am doing it for God."[56]

That is real faith, the kind of faith that results in love, obedience, and victory. That same faith can be ours as God works in us by the Holy Spirit.

Four Witnesses

Suppose you are a parent of a teenager and someone comes to you one day and tells you that your son or daughter was responsible for a hit and run accident. How would you respond?

For the sake of my illustration, let us also suppose that your son or daughter has not told you about the accident and that you do not know the person reporting this news to you.

I think that if I were the parent receiving this information from an unknown and unofficial source, I would certainly want to talk to my son about it and seek corroboration from other sources.

Now, what if my son denied being involved in the supposed hit and run accident, but the person who first reported this incident to me was able to take me to three other eye-witnesses who each saw my son commit the hit and run at a major intersection in town? Suppose further that each of these four witnesses were standing on a different corner of the intersection where the hit and run supposedly took place.

Barring some fanciful explanation for this occurrence, I think I would have to accept the witness of these four people, despite my son's denial, especially if these witnesses turned out to be trusted sources such as police officers or other upstanding citizens of the community.

I can assure you that nothing like this has ever happened in my family. I am simply using this story as a dramatic illustration of what John presents to us in this next section of his letter. John presents us with four witnesses who all testify, from different perspectives, that Jesus is the Christ, the Son of God, and that in Jesus there is life.

Many people long for assurance of the truth of their faith. That is exactly what John seeks to provide for us in 1 John 5:6-12....

> This is the one who came by water and blood—Jesus Christ. He did not come by water only, but by water and blood. And it is the Spirit who testifies, because the Spirit is the truth. For there are three that testify: the Spirit, the water and the blood; and the three are in agreement. We accept human testimony, but God's testimony is greater because it is the testimony of God, which he has given about his Son. Whoever believes in the Son of God accepts this testimony. Whoever does not believe

God has made him out to be a liar, because they have not believed the testimony God has given about his Son. And this is the testimony: God has given us eternal life, and this life is in his Son. Whoever has the Son has life; whoever does not have the Son of God does not have life.

The four witnesses to the central truth of the Christian faith that John marshals are these: the water, the blood, the Spirit, and the Son. Now, I will grant you that these witnesses can seem very obscure, unlike the four witnesses in my opening illustration. However, as we explore who or what each of these four witnesses are, I think you will see what John is getting at.

The first witness that John calls to the stand is the water. He says, "This is the one who came by water and blood—Jesus Christ. He did not come by water only, but by water and blood."

What is John talking about? How is water a witness to Jesus as the Christ, the Son of God?

Water has been interpreted as a reference to at least four different things down through the history of commentary on this passage. Some have interpreted the water mentioned here as a reference to Jesus' physical birth. However, we must remember that Jesus' physical birth was not a matter of dispute among the people John was writing to, nor was it a matter of dispute among the Gnostics whom John was writing against. Therefore, it seems unlikely that water refers to the water of Jesus' physical birth.

Others have taken water as a reference to Jesus' baptism. This seems much more likely. Jesus' baptism not only signaled the beginning of his public ministry, but it was also a time when there was divine witness to Jesus' identity. The Holy Spirit descended on Jesus in the form of a dove, and the voice of God affirmed that Jesus was God's beloved Son in whom God was well pleased (Mark 1:9-11).

Interestingly enough, the Gnostic teachers whom John was trying to combat agreed with him that Jesus came by water. However, the Gnostics put a different interpretive spin on the meaning of Jesus' baptism. The Gnostics viewed Jesus' baptism as the moment during which Jesus received the divine spirit as a *temporary* gift, whereas John viewed the gift of the Spirit to Jesus as something *permanent*. We will explore this further in a moment.

A third way people have interpreted the meaning of water in this passage is to say that it refers to the water that poured out of Jesus' side, along with blood, when the Roman soldier thrust his spear through Jesus while he was hanging on the cross.

It is quite likely that John did have this incident in mind. Whether or not the author of this letter and the author of the Gospel of John were the same person, it is quite clear that the author of this letter was very familiar with the Gospel of John. The author of this letter certainly was aware of the incident reported in John 19:34-35.

A fourth way that people have interpreted the meaning of water in this passage is to see it, along with the blood, as a foreshadowing of the two great sacraments of the church: baptism and the Lord's Supper. While this may be true, it does not fully account for John's use of the word "water" as a witness to Jesus as Messiah and Son of God.

Therefore, I think it best to view the water in this passage as a reference to Jesus' baptism, but there is a connection to our baptism as well.

I think we can understand how Jesus' baptism stands as a testimony to his divine identity. The dove descending and the voice from heaven saying, "This is my beloved son in whom I am well pleased" provide a vivid witness to Jesus as the Christ, the Son of God.

However, you might ask, "What difference does that make to me?"

That is a valid question. I believe it is only when we become personally identified with Jesus that this witness to Jesus' identity has any meaning for us.

One of the most interesting descriptions of the Christian in the New Testament is to say that the Christian is "in Christ". Paul says in 2 Corinthians 5:17, "Therefore, if anyone is *in Christ* that person is a new creation. The old has gone, the new is here!"

How do we end up "in Christ"?

It happens through faith. It happens through baptism. The acts of faith and of baptism identify us with Jesus Christ.

Furthermore, once we are "in Christ" what God says of his Son Jesus can also be said of us. If you have been baptized into Jesus Christ, if you have put your faith in him, then God is saying to you today, "You are my beloved son. You are my beloved daughter. In you I am well pleased." When we have that kind of experience of God's grace and love through Christ, it is a tremendous witness to Jesus' identity.

The second witness John calls to the stand to testify to the identity of Jesus as Messiah and Son of God is the blood. John says, "This is the one who came by water and blood—Jesus Christ. He did not come by water only, but by water and blood."

As I have already pointed out, the Gnostics would have agreed with John that Jesus came by water. The Gnostics believed that Jesus was indeed given the Holy Spirit at his baptism. However, the Gnostics also believed that the Holy Spirit left Jesus before his death. The Gnostics could not understand how the divine would associate himself with anything as ignominious as death.

However, this is the very point that John is at pains to stress. Jesus came not only by water but also by blood. Jesus was as much the Son of God, endowed with the Spirit, at his death as he was at his baptism. This is the essence and amazing nature of the atonement: that God took our death upon himself in Jesus on the cross.

How does the blood of Jesus testify to his identity as Messiah and Son of God? There was something about the way in which Jesus died that certified his identity even to a Roman centurion. In Mark 15:39 we read, "And when the centurion, who stood there in front of Jesus, saw how he died, he said, 'Surely this man was the Son of God!'"

Tom Wright says of this passage in 1 John, "No other god, no other power, no other being in all the world loves like this, gives like this, dies like this. All others win victories by fighting; this one, by suffering. All other gods exercise power by killing; this one, by dying."

Thus, we can understand in some measure why the death of Jesus was important, but why was the shedding of his blood necessary, and so much blood at that? Surely there have been many people, perhaps the majority in the history of the world, who have died without actually shedding blood. Why so much blood connected with the death of Jesus?

Certainly, from a human standpoint the answer is that Jesus shed so much blood because he was subjected to one of the most horrendous forms of execution devised by human beings. However, the shedding of blood was also spiritually significant from a Jewish standpoint.

Paul says, "The wages of sin is death." (Romans 3:23) When we turn away from God who is life, the only thing waiting for us is death. The only way to reverse this process is by an innocent person taking our death upon himself. The problem is that there has never been a completely innocent person in the history of humanity. That is, there has never been a thoroughly good and perfect person until God became a human being in Jesus of Nazareth. In him, we finally see perfect humanity. And that perfect human being did indeed take our death upon himself. Furthermore, because he was divine as well as human, his sacrifice was sufficient to cover over all our sin.

All through the history of the Jews recounted in the Hebrew Scriptures, there is an untold amount of blood shed through animal sacrifices. However, the problem was that these sacrifices only temporarily covered over sins. The sacrifices had to be constantly repeated.

Jesus died at Passover, a Jewish festival in which there were countless lambs sacrificed and much blood shed. John the Baptist made the connection between Jesus' death and the Passover when he said, "Behold the Lamb of God who takes away the sins of the world." (John 1:29) The visual connection between the profuse blood shed in animal sacrifice and the tremendous amount of blood shed in Jesus' suffering and crucifixion should have been clear to any Jew. The big difference is that once Jesus shed his blood for our sins that sacrifice did not need to be repeated. As it says in Hebrews 7:27…

> Unlike the other high priests, he does not need to offer sacrifices day after day, first for his own sins, and then for the sins of the people. He sacrificed for their sins once for all when he offered himself.

To the Jew, life was in the blood. The shedding of blood certified death. Thus, when blood and water came out of Jesus' side it certified that he had really died and thus his sacrifice was complete.

How does Jesus' shed blood act as a testimony to his identity today? I believe we receive confirmation of Jesus' identity and what he can do for us, forgiving our sins through his sacrifice, every time we receive the wine of the Lord's Supper and are reminded of the words of Jesus, "This is my blood of the covenant, which is poured out for many for the forgiveness of sins." (Matthew 26:28) As Paul says, whenever we eat the bread and drink the cup we proclaim Jesus' death until he comes again. (1 Corinthians 11:26)

The third witness John calls to the stand to testify to the identity of Jesus is the Spirit.

> And it is the Spirit who testifies, because the Spirit is the truth. For there are three that testify: the Spirit, the water and the blood; and the three are in agreement.

The Holy Spirit testified to the divine nature of Jesus when he descended upon Jesus out of the heavens in the form of a dove at Jesus' baptism. However, that is not all, because the Holy Spirit continues to testify to Jesus' identity to this day.

Jesus himself promised his first disciples, as recorded in John 15:26-27,

> When the Advocate comes, whom I will send to you from the Father—the Spirit of truth who goes out from the Father—he will testify about me. And you also must testify, for you have been with me from the beginning.

Then, a little bit later, in John 16:13, we read the words of Jesus:

> But when he, the Spirit of truth, comes, he will guide you into all the truth. He will not speak on his own; he will speak only what he hears, and he will tell you what is yet to come.

Thus, the Holy Spirit was promised to the first disciples. The Spirit testified through their preaching and through their writing, which we now have contained in the New Testament. Furthermore, I believe the Holy Spirit continues to testify to Jesus through the testimony of the apostles in the New Testament and through the faithful preaching of the Scriptures.

John goes on to tell us that these three witnesses (the water, the blood and the Spirit) are in agreement. Three witnesses in agreement in a court of law would provide the strongest testimony possible. So it is with the water, the blood and the Spirit; they provide the strongest testimony possible to the nature of Jesus as the Christ, the Son of God. John, in effect, asks us: "If we accept the testimony of human beings, why do we not accept the testimony of God to his only Son? After all, God's testimony is greater than that of any human being or collection of human beings."

When we believe in the Son of God, we accept God's testimony about his Son. Believing in the Son of God means more than just believing certain facts or statements about Jesus. It means entrusting our lives to his hands. John says that if we are not willing to do this, then we make God out to be a liar, which is a very serious action indeed.

As if the testimony of these three witnesses was not enough to convince us to commit our lives to following Jesus, God has also provided a fourth witness: the Son himself.

In a sense, this fourth witness is internal whereas the other three witnesses (the water, the blood and the Spirit) are external to us. John says, "He who is believing in the Son of God has the testimony in himself."

If the only witness we had to the person and work of Jesus of Nazareth was internal then non-Christians would have every right to say that we are deluding ourselves. That is why it is so important that we have both external, historical witnesses to the reality of who Jesus was and what he did two thousand years ago, as well as the internal witness. David Jackman puts it this way:

> It is as we meet the historical Jesus, through the apostolic testimony and the work of the Spirit, that the objective realities of all that he accomplished for us in his death and resurrection become internalized in our experience now. The new birth takes place and following it there develops the growing inner conviction that these things are true and they are true in and for us as individuals.

What is the testimony we have within ourselves? John explains:

> And this is the testimony: God has given us eternal life, and this life is in his Son. Whoever has the Son has life; whoever does not have the Son of God does not have life.

The testimony is eternal life, not just everlasting life, but an entirely new quality of life that begins the moment we believe in Jesus and will never end. Whoever has the Son has this life, and whoever does not have the Son (John probably has the Gnostics in mind) does not have life. Thus, the inner testimony that we have in our hearts is the Son, Jesus himself, living in us by his Holy Spirit. I cannot prove to you that Jesus lives in me, or in you, or in anyone else. However, if what John says is true, this has to be one of the most amazing truths ever revealed to human beings.

Reflections on I John

There have been many people over the course of the last two thousand years who have tried to disprove Jesus as Messiah and Son of God. Lew Wallace was one of these. He was the Governor of New Mexico over a century ago and here is what he wrote about his experience....

> I had always been an agnostic and denied Christianity. Robert C. Ingersoll, a famous agnostic, was one of my most intimate friends. He once suggested, "See here, Wallace, you are a learned man and a thinker. Why don't you gather material and write a book to prove the falsity concerning Jesus Christ, that no such man has ever lived, much less the author of the teachings found in the New Testament. Such a book would make you famous. It would be a masterpiece, and a way of putting an end to the foolishness about the so-called Christ."
>
> The thought made a deep impression on me, and we discussed the possibility of such a book. I went to Indianapolis, my home, and told my wife what I intended. She was a member of the Methodist Church and naturally did not like my plan. But I decided to do it and began to collect material in libraries here and in the old world. I gathered everything over that period in which Jesus Christ, according to legend, should have lived.
>
> Several years were spent in this work. I had written nearly four chapters when it became clear to me that Jesus Christ was just as real a personality as Socrates, Plato, or Caesar. The conviction became a certainty. I knew that Jesus Christ had lived because of the facts connected with the period in which he lived.
>
> I was in an uncomfortable position. I had begun to write a book to prove that Jesus Christ had never lived on earth. Now I was face to face with the fact that he was just as historic a personage as Julius Caesar, Mark Antony, Virgil, Dante, and a host of other men who had lived in olden days. I asked myself candidly, "If he was a real person (and there was no doubt), was he not then also the Son of God and the Savior of the world?" Gradually the consciousness grew that, since Jesus Christ was a real person, he probably was the one he claimed to be.
>
> I fell on my knees to pray for the first time in my life, and I asked God to reveal himself to me, forgive my sins, and help me to become a follower of Christ.

Lew Wallace did go on to write a book based upon his research, but it was very different from the one he originally planned.[57] I recently watched a remake of the movie based upon that book, *Ben Hur*. How encouraging it is to know that story was written by a man who wanted to disprove that Jesus ever existed, and instead became convinced that Jesus was and is the Messiah, the Son of God.

The witnesses testifying to the identity of Jesus that we have examined today are just four of many. When it comes to examining the evidence for the identity of Jesus of Nazareth, we all need to be like Lew Wallace, searching diligently for the truth. After all, God promises, "You will seek me and find me when you seek me with all your heart." (Jeremiah 29:13)

The Benefits of Being a Christian

Wilfredo Garza lived the life of an illegal immigrant for more than 35 years. Year after year, he eked out a living crossing the border from Mexico into the United States—some days finding work, some days not. Regardless, he was constantly looking over his shoulder. He was caught by the Border Patrol four times during that period and bused back to Mexico every time. Undeterred by each apprehension, he swam back across the Rio Grande to try again.

The cycle would likely have continued for several more years if not for an amazing discovery. One day, Wilfredo worked up the courage to walk into an immigration lawyer's office. There, incredibly, he found out that his father was born in Texas and spent time working there, which meant that Wilfredo was actually a U.S. citizen.

For more than 35 years, Wilfredo Garza could have possessed the very papers—his father's birth certificate and work records—that proved his citizenship, and yet he lived in guilt and fear. Now he has a certificate of citizenship. Now he does not have to sneak across the border; he can walk through the main gate.[58]

Many of us live like Wilfredo Garza, spiritually speaking. We have a tremendous citizenship, great privileges and benefits, but we do not realize it. Instead, we act like spiritual illegal aliens. God does not want us to live like that. God wants us to know that we belong to him and that he loves us. He wants us to know all the benefits of being his sons and daughters.

In this final section of his first letter, John tells us all about the benefits of being a Christian. Let's look one last time at what he has to say in 1 John 5:13-21....

> I write these things to you who believe in the name of the Son of God so that you may know that you have eternal life. This is the confidence we have in approaching God: that if we ask anything according to his will, he hears us. And if we know that he hears us—whatever we ask—we know that we have what we asked of him.
>
> If you see any brother or sister commit a sin that does not lead to death, you should pray and God will give them life. I refer to those whose sin does not lead to death. There is a sin that leads to death. I am not saying

that you should pray about that. All wrongdoing is sin, and there is sin that does not lead to death.

We know that anyone born of God does not continue to sin; the One who was born of God keeps them safe, and the evil one cannot harm them. We know that we are children of God, and that the whole world is under the control of the evil one. We know also that the Son of God has come and has given us understanding, so that we may know him who is true. And we are in him who is true by being in his Son Jesus Christ. He is the true God and eternal life.

Dear children, keep yourselves from idols.

In this conclusion to his first letter, John tells us about five benefits of being a Christian. The first is *assurance of salvation*.

John sums up the purpose of his letter by saying: "I write these things to you who believe in the name of the Son of God so that you may *know* that you have eternal life."

If we believe in the name of the Son of God, we can be certain that we have eternal life. That is one of the greatest benefits of being a Christian.

Believing in the name of the Son of God means: believing in everything that his name, Jesus, stands for. Jesus means "Yahweh saves". Have you entrusted your life to Jesus' care? Have you put your life in his hands? If so, then you can be sure that you have eternal life, not simply a life that will never end. Everlasting life will be miserable unless it is a life lived in God and in his Son Jesus Christ. Eternal life is an entirely new quality of life that God gives to us the moment we believe in his Son. William Barclay describes it this way:

> In God there is peace and, therefore, eternal life means serenity. It means a life liberated from the fears which haunt the human situation. In God there is power and, therefore, eternal life means the defeat of frustration. It means a life filled with the power of God and, therefore, victorious over circumstance. In God there is holiness and, therefore, eternal life means the defeat of sin. It means a life clad with the purity of God and armed against the soiling infections of the world. In God there is love and, therefore, eternal life means the end of bitterness and hatred. It means a life which has the love of God in its heart and the undefeatable love of man in all its feelings and in all its action. In God there is life and, therefore, eternal life means the defeat of death. It means a life which is indestructible because it has in it the indestructibility of God himself.

In every other religion, human beings try to reach up and grab hold of God. However, in Jesus Christ, God has reached down to us as struggling human beings and he says, "Here, let me help you." Other religions say: "Do!"

Reflections on I John

Christianity says: "Done!" Because that is so, Christians possess an assurance of salvation like no one else.

Tony Campolo shared the following story in a sermon a number of years ago....

> I went to my first black funeral when I was 16 years old. A friend of mine, Clarence, had died. The pastor was incredible. From the pulpit he talked about the Resurrection in beautiful terms. He had us thrilled. He came down from the pulpit, went to the family, and comforted them from the fourteenth chapter of John. "Let not your heart be troubled," he said, "'You believe in God, believe also in me,' said Jesus. Clarence has gone to heavenly mansions."
>
> Then, for the last 20 minutes of the sermon, he actually preached to the open casket. Now, that's drama! He yelled at the corpse: "Clarence! Clarence!" He said it with such authority. I would not have been surprised had there been an answer. He said, "Clarence, there were a lot of things we should have said to you that we never said to you. You got away too fast, Clarence. You got away too fast." He went down this litany of beautiful things that Clarence had done for people. When he finished—here's the dramatic part—he said, "That's it, Clarence. There's nothing more to say. When there's nothing more to say, there's only one thing to say. Good night. Good night, Clarence!" He grabbed the lid of the casket and slammed it shut. "Good night, Clarence!" Boom!
>
> Shock waves went over the congregation. As the preacher then lifted his head, you could see there was this smile on his face. He said, "Good night, Clarence. Good night, Clarence, because I know, I know that God is going to give you a good morning!" The choir stood and started singing, "On that great morning, we shall rise, we shall rise." We were dancing in the aisles and hugging each other. I knew the joy of the Lord, a joy that in the face of death laughs and sings and dances, for there is no sting to death.[59]

Now that is assurance! Where else can one get that kind of assurance of salvation but in Jesus Christ?

The second benefit John mentions that comes to the Christian is *confidence in prayer*.

This is the confidence we have in approaching God: that if we ask anything according to his will, he hears us. And if we know that he hears us—whatever we ask—we know that we have what we asked of him.

The word for confidence literally means "freedom of speech". As Christians, we have freedom of speech before the throne of our heavenly father. We can approach him at any time of night or day. Furthermore, if we ask for anything according to his will, we can know with certainty that God hears us. John is not talking about God's secret will that we cannot know, but rather God's moral will expressed in Scripture. Thus, if we ask for things God has promised to give to his children, we can know, not only that he hears us, but also that God will give us what we ask of him.

For example, 1 Timothy 2:4 says that God wants all people to be saved and come to a knowledge of the truth. George Mueller, who spent a lifetime caring for orphans, prayed for sixty-three years and eight months for the conversion of a particular friend. Late in life Mueller said, "He is not converted yet, but he will be! How can it be otherwise? There is the unchanging promise of Jehovah, and on that I rest." When Mueller died, his friend was still not a committed follower of Jesus Christ. However, before Mueller's body was buried, that friend came to faith.

As believers in Jesus Christ, we can have confidence in prayer.

A third benefit of the Christian life is *power over sin*.

One particular thing we can and should pray for as Christians is for our fellow believers who may be wandering from the Lord. John says,

> If you see any brother or sister commit a sin that does not lead to death, you should pray and God will give them life. I refer to those whose sin does not lead to death. There is a sin that leads to death. I am not saying that you should pray about that. All wrongdoing is sin, and there is sin that does not lead to death.

There has been much speculation over the last two thousand years about what the sin is that leads to death. Many Christians worry that they may have committed the unforgiveable sin, or the sin that leads to death. I can tell you one thing for sure, if you are worried that you have committed the sin that leads to death, then you have not committed it! I believe the sin that leads to death is the sin of refusing God's grace and forgiveness through Jesus Christ. If we refuse God's offer of grace, then there is nothing left for us but death.

The good news is that we serve the God of the second chance. God is always giving us more opportunities to receive his grace. Think of Peter. He denied three times even knowing Jesus on the night of Jesus' arrest. However, Jesus subsequently gave to Peter three chances to re-affirm his love for him. Jesus restored Peter in such a way that Peter became one of the greatest leaders of the early church. If the Lord did that much for Peter, surely he will do that much and perhaps even more for us.

The bottom line is that God gives to every Christian through his Son and the Spirit, power over sin. John says,

> We know that anyone born of God does not continue to sin; the One

who was born of God keeps them safe, and the evil one cannot harm them.

Now, obviously, as we saw in 1 John 1, Christians *do* sin. What John means by Christians *not continuing to sin* is that our lives are not *characterized* by sin; they are not *dominated* by it. Our Christian life may be one of three steps forward, two steps back, but we *are* making progress. That is true because the one who was born of God, Jesus Christ, keeps us safe, so that the evil one cannot harm us. We are no longer in the grasp of Satan, but rather, in the everlasting arms of our faithful God.

By contrast, James 1:14-15 describes our typical downward spiral,

> Each person is tempted when they are dragged away by their own evil desire and enticed. Then, after desire has conceived, it gives birth to sin; and sin, when it is full-grown, gives birth to death.

Fritz Ridenour says we need to practice spiritual birth control. The question is: how? I think the story of Adolph Ochs gives us a clue.

Ochs was the publisher of the New York Times in the 1920s. Business was so bad that Ochs was known for saving a few cents by wandering through the office late at night and turning off lights. Then, in the midst of the newspaper's great financial struggle, a trusted friend offered Ochs a $150,000 advertising contract with "no strings attached". However, Ochs refused the offer, because he was afraid that if he accepted the contract he would become dependent on that one large account and thereby tempted to compromise the newspaper's integrity. Ochs cut off temptation at the pass.

Not only do we need to do the same thing, but God also gives us the power to do so. 1 Corinthians 10:13 says,

> No temptation has overtaken you except what is common to mankind. And God is faithful; he will not let you be tempted beyond what you can bear. But when you are tempted, he will also provide a way out so that you can endure it.

The fourth benefit of being a Christian that John mentions here is *a right attitude toward the world*.

John says, "We know that we are children of God, and that the whole world is under the control of the evil one."

This can sound perilously like John is saying, "We Christians are right, and everyone else is wrong!" However, is this what John is really saying?

Let us look at this statement piece by piece. The first part of the sentence stresses that God alone is the source of our life. This is actually a humble statement. All that we have comes from God and thus we belong to God entirely: in our bodies, minds, and spirits. By definition then, a Christian ought to act differently from the "world system" that is set against God.

In the second half of this statement, John tells us that the world system is under the control of the evil one. One only has to turn on the television or log on to the Internet to realize that Satan is doing a pretty good job of getting his message out to the world and dominating the world's thinking.

What is Satan's message? Jesus says in John 10:10, "The thief comes only to steal and kill and destroy; I have come that they may have life, and have it to the full."

If this is true, if those of us who are *in Christ* have life to the full, and if Satan is stealing from, killing, and destroying those under the domination of the world system, then what ought to be our attitude towards those who do not yet know Christ? Should our attitude not be one of wanting to share life in all its fullness? Should we not be like beggars telling other beggars where to get bread?

David Jackman says,

> What is inexcusable is for the church to concentrate on trying to preserve its distinctives in a hermetically sealed environment of detachment from the world and its problems. That is a luxury Christ has not afforded us. Indeed, it is not a luxury at all, but a quick route to death by suffocation. If we live under Christ's lordship we must remember that he has commissioned us all to go into the world, not to withdraw from it. Our new attitude is not one of indifference or separation, but one of involvement and compassion, after the model of our Saviour.

I saw an example of what our attitude toward the world should be when I logged on to Facebook one morning not too long ago. I have a friend on Facebook whose name is Paul Gurung. He is an evangelist in Nepal. A photo on Facebook showed Paul cleaning the wounds of street children who have many cuts on their feet because they walk around with no shoes. As Paul was cleaning the feet of these children, he was also praying for each child. Another photo showed him cutting the long hair of some street children, and again, while he was doing so, he was praying for each one. A third photo showed Paul and his team feeding the street children of Kalimati. The children were seated in rows on the sidewalk, each with a plate of food in front of them.

Three photos, three glimpses of what our life as Christians ought to be like in this world. Perhaps we cannot go to Nepal to feed the street children, to cut their hair and wash their feet. However, we certainly can support people like Paul Gurung who are doing this sort of work, and we can ask the Lord what needs he wants us to fill in the world right around us.

The final benefit of being a Christian that John talks about, as he wraps up his letter, is the benefit of *a new awareness of God*. John says,

> We know also that the Son of God has come and has given us understanding, so that we may know him who is true. And we are in him who is true by being in his Son Jesus Christ. He is the true God and eternal life.

Christian faith is grounded in history: the Son of God has come. Furthermore, Christ's coming has given us understanding, not primarily intellectual understanding, though it involves the intellect, but personal knowledge of him who is true, that is: God. We are *in* God by virtue of being *in* Jesus Christ, God's Son, and being *in* God means having eternal life.

However, John ends his letter on a curious note: "Dear children, keep yourselves from idols." Why does John end this great "love letter" in this seemingly strange fashion?

I think the reason is this: though our faith is grounded in history, our God is not one whom we can see at present. Therefore, it is all too easy for us as Christians to get frustrated with the mystery, to become impatient with our invisible God and long for a God whom we can see with our physical eyes, hear with our physical ears, and touch with our physical hands.

This is where idols come in. An idol is anything that occupies the place of God. An idol is an imitation, a substitute for God, not the reality. Down through history human beings have made idols of wood, stone or precious metals. Thus, we may tend to think we do not have idols because we do not bow down and worship such things.

However, what about power? What about money? What about sex? What about certain human relationships in our lives? Do not some of these tend to occupy the place of God for us? If so, then they are idols, and we need to remove them from the pedestals on which we place them, and put God back in the highest place. As David Jackman says, "Anything that squeezes God out of the central position towards the margin of my life must be ruthlessly toppled."

David Foster Wallace was an award-winning, best-selling novelist who committed suicide in 2008. Before his death, Wallace gave a commencement address in which he said this to the graduating class:

> In the day-to-day trenches of adult life, there is actually no such thing as atheism.... Everybody worships. The only choice we get is what to worship. And ... pretty much anything you worship will eat you alive. If you worship money and things—if they are where you tap real meaning in life—then you will never have enough.... Worship your own body and beauty and sexual allure and you will always feel ugly, and when time and age start showing, you will die a million deaths before they finally plant you.... Worship power—you will feel weak and afraid, and you will need ever more power over others to keep the

fear at bay. Worship your intellect, being seen as smart—you will end up feeling stupid, a fraud, always on the verge of being found out.⁶⁰

What is the alternative to worshipping idols and ending up broken, defeated and empty? The alternative is to turn to the one who promises to give us life and love, meaning and purpose, in all of their fullness.

Conclusion

C. S. Lewis once wrote,

> God, who needs nothing, loves into existence wholly superfluous creatures in order that He may love and perfect them. He creates the universe, already foreseeing—or should we say "seeing"? there are no tenses in God—the buzzing cloud of flies about the cross, the flayed back pressed against the uneven stake, the nails driven through the mesial nerves, the repeated incipient suffocation as the body droops, the repeated torture of back and arms as it is time after time, for breath's sake, hitched up. If I may dare the biological image, God is a "host" who deliberately creates His own parasites; causes us to be that we may exploit and "take advantage of" Him. Herein is love. This is the diagram of Love Himself, the inventor of all loves.[61]

Lewis sums up in 130 words what I have tried to say in over 55,000 words in this book. The message could actually be summed up in three words: God loves you.

Accepting that message, embracing it, really taking it to heart, changes life; it literally turns life upside down. The truth of God's love makes any pain bearable by his grace; it makes the heart sing, even in the hellish pits of this world.

Why would anyone reject such a love as this? The answer is perhaps: because love is risky. When we engage in love, as Lewis also says, we become vulnerable....

> To love at all is to be vulnerable. Love anything and your heart will be wrung and possibly broken. If you want to make sure of keeping it intact you must give it to no one, not even an animal. Wrap it carefully round with hobbies and little luxuries; avoid all entanglements. Lock it up safe in the casket or coffin of your selfishness. But in that casket, safe, dark, motionless, airless, it will change. It will not be broken; it will become unbreakable, impenetrable, irredeemable. The alternative to tragedy, or at least to the risk of tragedy, is damnation. The only place outside Heaven where you can be perfectly safe from all the dangers and perturbations of love is Hell.[62]

As uncomfortable as Lewis' statement may make us feel, I believe it is nonetheless true. We have, just as John told us almost two thousand years ago, a stark choice before us: love or hatred, light or dark, life or death, heaven or hell.

Moses once said to the people of Israel: "I have set before you life and death, blessings and curses. Now choose life…" (Deuteronomy 30:19)

I believe God also sets before each of us a similar choice every day. It is the choice between love or hatred, fullness or emptiness. And the Lord in his compassion and grace is quite clear about what he wants us to choose. He says to you and to me, this day and every day: "Therefore choose love!"

It is ours to answer, and upon that answer hangs our eternal destiny.

ENDNOTES

1 Jackman, David, *The Message of John's Letters*, Downer's Grove, Illinois: InterVarsity Press, 1988, p. 18.
2 Guthrie, Donald, *New Testament Introduction*, Downer's Grove, Illinois: InterVarsity Press, 1970, p. 864.
3 William D. Hendricks, *Exit Interviews (Chicago: Moody, 1993)*
4 Matt Woodley, managing editor, PreachingToday.com; sources: Madeline Levine, *The Price of Privilege* (Harper Perennial, 2008), pp. 3-5; Joy Lanzendorfer, "All and Nothing," Metro Active, (1-3-07)
5 Lewis, C. S., *The Weight of Glory*, New York: Macmillan, 1980, p. 92.
6 Hooper, Walter, *The Collected Letters of C. S. Lewis*, Volume II, New York: HarperCollins, 2004, p. 507.
7 Brian Coffey, from the sermon, *"How Bad Is Too Bad?" (2-24-02);* submitted by Kevin A. Miller, vice president, Christianity Today International preachingtoday.com
8 Matt Woodley, managing editor, *PreachingToday.com;* sources: John Cassian, *The Conferences (Newman Press, 1997), p. 91;* C.R. Snyder, *Coping With Stress (Oxford University Press, 2001), pp. 196-2*
9 Rebecca Pippert, *Hope Has Its Reasons* (InterVarsity Press, 2001), pp. 31-32
10 Zack Eswine, *Sensing Jesus* (Crossway, 2012), pp. 62-63.
11 Lee Eclov, Vernon Hills, Illinois; source: adapted from James Bryan Smith, *The Good and Beautiful God* (IVP, 2009), p. 142
12 Charles R. Swindoll in *Leadership, Vol. 8, no. 4.*
13 William Falk, *The Week (3-2-07),* p. 5; submitted by Ted DeHass, Bedford, Iowa, preachingtoday.com
14 Mark Buchanan, *Hidden in Plain Sight* (Thomas Nelson, 2007), pp. 187-189; submitted by Lee Eclov, Vernon Hills, Illinois
15 Ron Hutchcraft, *Living Peacefully in a Stressful World;* reprinted in *Men of Integrity* (Nov/Dec 2002)
16 *The Devil Wears Prada* (Fox Pictures, 2006), directed by David Frankel; submitted by John Beukema, Chambersburg, Pennsylvania, preachingtoday.com

17 Kristen Scharold, Wheaton, Illinois; source: Marcus Wohlsen, "Fish used to detect terror attacks," www.ABCNews.com (9-19-06)
18 "Steve Jobs Best Quotes," *The Wall Street Journal* (8-24-11)
19 "The Nature of Existence," DVD, directed by Roger Nygard, 2010, chapter 23: "Truth," 33:44 - 36:11; submitted by Jerry de Luca; West Montreal, Canada, preachingtoday.com
20 Michael Green, in Alice Gray's (editor) *Stories for a Faithful Heart* (Multnomah, 2004), p. 95; submitted by Lee Eclov, Vernon Hills, Illinois, preachingtoday.com
21 Bill Glass, "The Power of a Father's Blessing," *Christianity Today* (January 2006), p. 48.
22 *Parenthood*, Ron Howard, creator and executive producer, "One Step Forward, Two Steps Back," Season 4, Episode 14; submitted by Kevin Emmert, Wheaton, Illinois, preachingtoday.com
23 Earl Palmer, "The Foolish and the Wise," *Preaching Today*, Tape No. 54.
24 Len Sullivan, Tupelo, Mississippi, preachingtoday.com
25 C. S. Lewis, *Mere Christianity*, New York: Macmillan, 1984, p. 52.
26 "Discovery of Oxygen," http://www.juliantrubin.com; submitted to preachingtoday.com by Clark Cothern, Tecumseh, Michigan.
27 U2 (with Neil McCormick), U2 by U2 (HarperCollins, 2006), p. 7
28 Bill White, Paramount, California, submitted to preachingtoday.com
29 William Willimon, *Pastor: The Theology and Practice of Ordained Ministry*, (Abingdon Press, 2002), p. 53; submitted to preachingtoday.com by David Slagle, Wilmore, Kentucky
30 Paul Borthwick, "In Jesus' Name, Amen," *Christian Reader* (January/February 2001), p. 30-31
31 Steve DeNeff and David Drury, *Soul Shift* (Wesleyan Publishing House, 2011), p. 55
32 Jimmy Carter, *Sources of Strength, Meditations on Scripture for a Living Faith*, Times Books, 1997, p. xvii; submitted by Ted De to preachingtoday.com
33 Leonard Sweet, *The Gospel According to Starbucks* (Waterbrook Press, 2007), p. 54; submitted by David Slagle, Atlanta, Georgia, to preachingtoday.com.
34 C. S. Lewis, *Mere Christianity*, New York: Macmillan, 1984, p. 43.

35 Os Guinness, *Unspeakable*, New York: HarperCollins, 2005, pp. 144-145, accessed from preachingtoday.com.
36 Victor Pentz, from the sermon "The Gourmet God," delivered at Peachtree Presbyterian Church, Atlanta, Georgia (11-23-03) accessed on preachingtoday.com
37 "Napoleon Bonaparte," *Leadership*, Vol. 7, no. 1
38 "D.L. Moody," *Christian History*, no. 25.
39 *What Is Love—From a Kid's Point of View*, LightSinger, (accessed 3-14-02); submitted by Jerry De Luca, Montreal West, Quebec, preachingtoday.com
40 Belden Lane, "Rabbinical Stories," *Christian Century* 98:41 (12-16-81); submitted by Bill White, Paramount, California, preachingtoday.com
41 "Fred Rogers," *Christianity Today* (3-6-00), p.45
42 Les and Leslie Parrott, *Relationships* (Zondervan, 1998), p. 172
43 Canadian Edition, *Time* (11-23-02); submitted by Darin Latham, St. Catherines, Ontario, Canada, preachingtoday.com
44 Timothy Keller, *The Prodigal God* (Riverhead Books, 2008), pp. 96-98
45 John Trent, co-author of *The Hidden Value of a Man. Men of Integrity*, Vol. 1, no. 1
46 Daniel Gilbert, "What You Don't Know Makes You Nervous," (9-21-09); as seen in *The Week* magazine, (6-5-09), p. 14
47 Andrea Sands, Edmonton Sun (12-30-04); submitted by Kirk MacLeod, Keswick, Ontario, Canada, preachingtoday.com
48 Greg Huffer; Lebanon, Indiana; source: ABC, WRTV Indianapolis; Bill Melendez Productions, preachingtoday.com
49 Skye Jethani, *With* (Thomas H. Nelson, 2011), pp. 80-82
50 Eugene Peterson in *Living The Message. Christianity Today*, Vol. 40, no. 11.
51 Submitted by Phil LeMaster, Senior Minister, First Church of Christ, Grayson, Kentucky, preachingtoday.com
52 R. L. Russell, "Triumphing over Trials," *Preaching Today*, Tape No. 119.
53 Gordon Johnson, "Finding Significance in Obscurity," *Preaching Today*, Tape No. 82.
54 Mike Breaux, pastor of Heartland Community Church, Rockford, Illinois, in a sermon at Willow Creek Community Church (5-26-02).
55 Frederick Buechner, *Wishful Thinking: A Theological ABC*
56 Lyn Cryderman, *Christianity Today*, Nov. 20, 1987, submitted

by Don Maddox, Corona, CA, preachingtoday.com
57 David Holdaway, *The Life of Jesus* (Sovereign World, 1997), pp. 42-43.
58 Anderson Cooper, "360 Degrees, On the Border" (aired 5-25-06), CNN; submitted by Jay Caron, East Wenatchee, Washington, preachingtoday.com
59 Tony Campolo, in the sermon "The Year of Jubilee," PreachingToday.com
60 Adapted from Timothy Keller, *The Insider and the Outcast* (Dutton Adult, 2013); original source: David Foster Wallace, "David Foster Wallace on Life and Work," *The Wall Street Journal* (9-19-08)
61 C. S. Lewis, *The Four Loves*, San Diego: Harcourt Brace Jovanovich, 1960, p. 176.
62 Ibid, p. 169

For Further Reading

Allen, Diogenes, *Love: Christian Romance, Marriage, Friendship*, Cambridge, Massachusetts: Cowley Publications, 1987.

Barclay, William, *The Letters of John and Jude*, Louisville, Kentucky: Westminster John Knox Press, 2002.

Jackman, David, *The Message of John's Letters*, Downers Grove, Illinois: InterVarsity Press, 1988.

Lewis, C. S., *The Four Loves*, San Diego: Harcourt Brace Jovanovich, 1960.

Palmer, Earl, *Love Has Its Reasons*, Waco, Texas: Word Books, 1977.

Ridenour, Fritz, *How to Be a Christian Without Being Perfect*, Ventura, California: Regal Books, 1986.

Wright, N. T., *The Early Christian Letters for Everyone*, Louisville, Kentucky: Westminster John Knox Press, 2011.

ABOUT THE AUTHOR

WILL VAUS

- was born in Sleepy Hollow, New York and grew up in La Jolla, California.
- is the son of Jim Vaus, former organized crime wiretapper who came to Christ through the ministry of Billy Graham in 1949.
- holds a Bachelor of Arts degree in drama from the University of California at San Diego and a Master of Divinity degree from Princeton Theological Seminary.
- has served as a pastor in California, South Carolina and Pennsylvania.
- is the president of Will Vaus Ministries, through which he has communicated the love of Christ around the world since 1988.
- is the author of *Mere Theology: A Guide to the Thought of C. S. Lewis*, *My Father Was a Gangster: The Jim Vaus Story*, *The Professor of Narnia: The C. S. Lewis Story*, *Speaking of Jack: A C. S. Lewis Discussion Guide*, *The Hidden Story of Narnia: A Book-by-Book Guide to Lewis' Spiritual Themes*, *Keys To Growth: Meditations on the Acts of the Apostles*, *Open Before Christmas: Devotional Thoughts for the Holiday Season*, and *Sheldon Vanauken: The Man Who Received a Severe Mercy*.
- and his wife, Becky, have been married since 1988 and have three sons: James, Jonathan and Joshua.
- has a website you can visit: www.willvaus.com

OTHER BOOKS OF INTEREST

C. S. Lewis

C. S. Lewis: Views From Wake Forest - Essays on C. S. Lewis
Michael Travers, editor

Contains sixteen scholarly presentations from the international C. S. Lewis convention in Wake Forest, NC. Walter Hooper shares his important essay "Editing C. S. Lewis," a chronicle of publishing decisions after Lewis' death in 1963.

"Scholars from a variety of disciplines address a wide range of issues. The happy result is a fresh and expansive view of an author who well deserves this kind of thoughtful attention."
  Diana Pavlac Glyer, author of *The Company They Keep*

The Hidden Story of Narnia:
A Book-By-Book Guide to Lewis' Spiritual Themes
Will Vaus

A book of insightful commentary equally suited for teens or adults – Will Vaus points out connections between the *Narnia* books and spiritual/biblical themes, as well as between ideas in the *Narnia* books and C. S. Lewis' other books. Learn what Lewis himself said about the overarching and unifying thematic structure of the Narnia books. That is what this book explores; what C. S. Lewis called "the hidden story" of Narnia. Each chapter includes questions for individual use or small group discussion.

Why I Believe in Narnia:
33 Reviews and Essays on the Life and Work of C.S. Lewis
James Como

Chapters range from reviews of critical books , documentaries and movies to evaluations of Lewis' books to biographical analysis.
"A valuable, wide-ranging collection of essays by one of the best informed and most acute commentators on Lewis' work and ideas."
  Peter Schakel, author of *Imagination & the Arts in C.S. Lewis*

Shadows and Chivalry:
C.S. Lewis and George MacDonald on Suffering, Evil, and Death
Jeff McInnis

Shadows and Chivalry studies the influence of George MacDonald, a nineteenth-century Scottish novelist and fantasy writer, upon one of the most influential writers of modern times, C. S. Lewis—the creator of Narnia, literary critic, and best-selling apologist. This study attempts to trace the overall affect of MacDonald's work on Lewis's thought and imagination. Without ever ceasing to be a story of one man's influence upon another, the study also serves as an exploration of each writer's thought on, and literary visions of, good and evil.

C. S. Lewis Goes to Heaven: A Reader's Guide to The Great Divorce
David G. Clark

This is the first book devoted solely to this often neglected book and the first to reveal several important secrets Lewis concealed within the story. Lewis felt his imaginary trip to Hell and Heaven was far better than his book *The Screwtape Letters*, which has become a classic. Clark has taught courses on Lewis for more than 30 years and is a New Testament and Greek scholar with a Doctor of Philosophy degree in Biblical Studies. Readers will discover the many literary and biblical influences Lewis utilized in writing his brilliant novel.

C. S. Lewis & Philosophy as a Way of Life: His Philosophical Thoughts
Adam Barkman

C. S. Lewis is rarely thought of as a "philosopher" per se despite having both studied and taught philosophy for several years at Oxford. Lewis's long journey to Christianity was essentially philosophical – passing through seven different stages. This 624 page book is an invaluable reference for C. S. Lewis scholars and fans alike

C. S. Lewis: His Literary Achievement
Colin Manlove

"This is a positively brilliant book, written with splendor, elegance, profundity and evidencing an enormous amount of learning. This is probably not a book to give a first-time reader of Lewis. But for those who are more broadly read in the Lewis corpus this book is an absolute gold mine of information. The author gives us a magnificent overview of Lewis' many writings, tracing for us thoughts and ideas which recur throughout, and at the same time telling us how each book differs from the others. I think it is not extravagant to call C. S. Lewis: His Literary Achievement a tour de force."

Robert Merchant, *St. Austin Review*, Book Review Editor

Mythopoeic Narnia: Memory, Metaphor, and Metamorphoses in C. S. Lewis's The Chronicles of Narnia
Salwa Khoddam

Dr. Khoddam offers a fresh approach to the *Narnia* books based on an inquiry into Lewis' readings and use of classical and Christian symbols. She explores the literary and intellectual contexts of these stories, the traditional myths and motifs, and places them in the company of the greatest Christian mythopoeic works of Western Literature. In Lewis' imagination, memory and metaphor interact to advance his purpose – a Christian metamorphosis. *Mythopoeic Narnia* opens the door for readers into the magical world of the Western imagination.

Speaking of Jack: A C. S. Lewis Discussion Guide
Will Vaus

C. S. Lewis Societies have been forming around the world since the first one started in New York City in 1969. Will Vaus has started and led three groups himself. *Speaking of Jack* is the result of Vaus' experience in leading those Lewis Societies. Included here are introductions to most of Lewis' books as well as questions designed to stimulate discussion about Lewis' life and work. These materials have been "road-tested" with real groups made up of young and old, some very familiar with Lewis and some newcomers. *Speaking of Jack* may be used in an existing book discussion group, to start a C. S. Lewis Society, or as a guide to your own exploration of Lewis' books.

George MacDonald

Diary of an Old Soul & The White Page Poems
George MacDonald and Betty Aberlin

The first edition of George MacDonald's book of daily poems included a blank page opposite each page of poems. Readers were invited to write their own reflections on the "white page." MacDonald wrote: "Let your white page be ground, my print be seed, growing to golden ears, that faith and hope may feed." Betty Aberlin responded to MacDonald's invitation with daily poems of her own.

Betty Aberlin's close readings of George MacDonald's verses and her thoughtful responses to them speak clearly of her poetic gifts and spiritual intelligence.
      Luci Shaw, poet

George MacDonald: Literary Heritage and Heirs
Roderick McGillis, editor

This latest collection of 14 essays sets a new standard that will influence MacDonald studies for many more years. George MacDonald experts are increasingly evaluating his entire corpus within the nineteenth century context.

This comprehensive collection represents the best of contemporary scholarship on George MacDonald.
      Rolland Hein, author of *George MacDonald: Victorian Mythmaker*

In the Near Loss of Everything: George MacDonald's Son in America
Dale Wayne Slusser

In the summer of 1887, George MacDonald's son Ronald, newly engaged to artist Louise Blandy, sailed from England to America to teach school. The next summer he returned to England to marry Louise and bring her back to America. On August 27, 1890, Louise died leaving him with an infant daughter. Ronald once described losing a beloved spouse as "the near loss of everything". Dale Wayne Slusser unfolds this poignant story with unpublished letters and photos that give readers a glimpse into the close-knit MacDonald family. Also included is Ronald's essay about his father, *George MacDonald: A Personal Note*, plus a selection from Ronald's 1922 fable, *The Laughing Elf*, about the necessity of both sorrow and joy in life.

A Novel Pulpit: Sermons From George MacDonald's Fiction
David L. Neuhouser

Each of the sermons has an introduction giving some explanation of the setting of the sermon or of the plot, if that is necessary for understanding the sermon. *"MacDonald's novels are both stimulating and thought-provoking. This collection of sermons from ten novels serve to bring out the 'freshness and brilliance' of MacDonald's message." from the author's introduction*

Behind the Back of the North Wind: Essays on George MacDonald's Classic Book
Edited and with Introduction by John Pennington and Roderick McGillis

The unique blend of fairy tale atmosphere and social realism in this novel laid the groundwork for modern fantasy literature. Sixteen essays by various authors are accompanied by an instructive introduction, extensive index, and beautiful illustrations.

Through the Year with George MacDonald: 366 Daily Readings
Rolland Hein, editor

These page-length excerpts from sermons, novels and letters are given an appropriate theme/heading and a complementary Scripture passage for daily reading. An inspiring introduction to the artistic soul and Christian vision of George MacDonald.

Poets and Poetry

Remembering Roy Campbell: The Memoirs of his Daughters, Anna and Tess
Introduction by Judith Lütge Coullie, Editor
Preface by Joseph Pearce

Anna and Teresa Campbell were the daughters of the handsome young South African poet and writer, Roy Campbell (1901-1957), and his beautiful English wife, Mary Garman. In their frank and moving memoirs, Anna and Tess recall the extraordinary, and often very difficult, lives they shared with their exceptional parents. Over 50 photos, 344 footnotes, timeline of Campbell's life, and complete index.

In the Eye of the Beholder: How to See the World Like a Romantic Poet
Louis Markos

Born out of the French Revolution and its radical faith that a nation could be shaped and altered by the dreams and visions of its people, British Romantic Poetry was founded on a belief that the objects and realities of our world, whether natural or human, are not fixed in stone but can be molded and transformed by the visionary eye of the poet. A separate bibliographical essay is provided for readers listing accessible biographies of each poet and critical studies of their work.

The Cat on the Catamaran: A Christmas Tale
John Martin

Here is a modern-day parable of a modern-day cat with modern-day attitudes. Riverboat Dan is a "cool" cat on a perpetual vacation from responsibility. He's *The Cat on the Catamaran* – sailing down the river of life. Dan keeps his guilty conscience from interfering with his fun until he runs into trouble. But will he have the courage to believe that it's never too late to change course? (For ages 10 to adult)

"*Cat lovers and poetry lovers alike will enjoy this whimsical story about Riverboat Dan, a philosophical cat in search of meaning.*"
           Regina Doman, author of *Angel in the Water*

The Half Blood Poems
Inspired by the Stories of J.K. Rowling
Christine Lowther

Like Harry Potter, Christine's poetry can soar above the tragic to discover the heroic and beautiful in such poems as "Neville, Unlikely Rebel", "For Our Wide-Armed Mothers," and "A Boy's Hands." There are 71 poems divided into seven chapters that correspond to the seven books. Fans of Harry Potter will experience once again many of the emotions they felt reading the books – emotions presented most effectively through a poet's words.

Pop Culture

To Love Another Person: A Spiritual Journey Through Les Miserables
John Morrison

The powerful story of Jean Valjean's redemption is beloved by readers and theater goers everywhere. In this companion and guide to Victor Hugo's masterpiece, author John Morrison unfolds the spiritual depth and breadth of this classic novel and broadway musical.

Through Common Things: Philosophical Reflections on Popular Culture
Adam Barkman

"Barkman presents us with an amazingly wide-ranging collection of philosophical reflections grounded in the everyday things of popular culture – past and present, eastern and western, factual and fictional. Throughout his encounters with often surprising subject-matter (the value of darkness?), he writes clearly and concisely, moving seamlessly between Aristotle and anime, Lord Buddha and Lord Voldemort.... This is an informative and entertaining book to read!"
  Doug Bloomberg, Professor of Philosophy, Institute for Christian Studies

Spotlight:
A Close-up Look at the Artistry and Meaning of Stephenie Meyer's Twilight Novels
John Granger

Stephenie Meyer's *Twilight* saga has taken the world by storm. But is there more to *Twilight* than a love story for teen girls crossed with a cheesy vampire-werewolf drama? *Spotlight* reveals the literary backdrop, themes, artistry, and meaning of the four Bella Swan adventures. *Spotlight* is the perfect gift for serious *Twilight* readers.

Virtuous Worlds: The Video Gamer's Guide to Spiritual Truth
John Stanifer

Popular titles like *Halo 3* and *The Legend of Zelda: Twilight Princess* fly off shelves at a mind-blowing rate. John Stanifer, an avid gamer, shows readers specific parallels between Christian faith and the content of their favorite games. Written with wry humor (including a heckler who frequently pokes fun at the author) this book will appeal to gamers and non-gamers alike. Those unfamiliar with video games may be pleasantly surprised to find that many elements in those "virtual worlds" also qualify them as "virtuous worlds."

The Many Faces of Katniss Everdeen: Exploring the Heroine of The Hunger Games
Valerie Estelle Frankel

Katniss is the heroine who's changed the world. Like Harry Potter, she explodes across genres: She is a dystopian heroine, a warrior woman, a reality TV star, a rebellious adolescent. She's surrounded by the figures of Roman history, from Caesar and Cato to Cinna and Coriolanus Snow. She's also traveling the classic heroine's journey. As a child soldier, she faces trauma; as a growing teen, she battles through love triangles and the struggle to be good in a harsh world. This book explores all this and more, while taking a look at the series' symbolism, from food to storytelling, to show how Katniss becomes the greatest power of Panem, the girl on fire.

Memoir

Called to Serve: Life as a Firefighter-Deacon
Deacon Anthony R. Surozenski

Called to Serve is the story of one man's dream to be a firefighter. But dreams have a way of taking detours – so Tony Soruzenski became a teacher and eventually a volunteer firefighter. And when God enters the picture, Tony is faced with a choice. Will he give up firefighting to follow another call? After many years, Tony's two callings are finally united – in service as a fire chaplain at Ground Zero after the 9-11 attacks and in other ways he could not have imagined. Tony is Chief Chaplain's aid for the Massachusettes Corp of Fire Chaplains and Director for the Office of the Diaconate of the Diocese of Worchester, Massachusettes.

Biography

Sheldon Vanauken: The Man Who Received "A Severe Mercy"
Will Vaus

In this biography we discover: Vanauken the struggling student, the bon-vivant lover, the sailor who witnessed the bombing of Pearl Harbor, the seeker who returned to faith through C. S. Lewis, the beloved professor of English literature and history, the feminist and anti-war activist who participated in the March on the Pentagon, the bestselling author, and Vanauken the convert to Catholicism. What emerges is the portrait of a man relentlessly in search of beauty, love, and truth, a man who believed that, in the end, he found all three.

"This is a charming biography about a doubly charming man who wrote a triply charming book. It is a great way to meet the man behind A Severe Mercy."

>   Peter Kreeft, author of *Jacob's Ladder: 10 Steps to Truth*

Fiction

The Iona Conspiracy (from The Remnant Chronicles book series)
Gary Gregg

Readers find themselves on a modern adventure through ancient Celtic myth and legend as thirteen year old Jacob uncovers his destiny within "the remnant" of the Sporrai Order. As the Iona Academy comes under the control of educational reformers and ideological scientists, Jacob finds himself on a dangerous mission to the sacred Scottish island of Iona and discovers how his life is wrapped up with the fate of the long lost cover of *The Book of Kells*. From its connections to Arthurian legend to references to real-life people, places, and historical mysteries, *Iona* is an adventure that speaks to eternal truths as well as the challenges of the modern world. A young adult novel, *Iona* can be enjoyed by the entire family.

Harry Potter

The Order of Harry Potter: The Literary Skill of the Hogwarts Epic
Colin Manlove

Colin Manlove, a popular conference speaker and author of over a dozen books, has earned an international reputation as an expert on fantasy and children's literature. His book, *From Alice to Harry Potter*, is a survey of 400 English fantasy books. In *The Order of Harry Potter*, he compares and contrasts *Harry Potter* with works by "Inklings" writers J.R.R. Tolkien, C.S. Lewis and Charles Williams; he also examines Rowling's treatment of the topic of imagination; her skill in organization and the use of language; and the book's underlying motifs and themes.

Harry Potter & Imagination: The Way Between Two Worlds
Travis Prinzi

Imaginative literature places a reader between two worlds: the story world and the world of daily life, and challenges the reader to imagine and to act for a better world. Starting with discussion of Harry Potter's more important themes, *Harry Potter & Imagination* takes readers on a journey through the transformative power of those themes for both the individual and for culture by placing Rowling's series in its literary, historical, and cultural contexts.

Repotting Harry Potter: A Professor's Guide for the Serious Re-Reader
Rowling Revisited: Return Trips to Harry, Fantastic Beasts, Quidditch, & Beedle the Bard
Dr. James W. Thomas

In *Repotting Harry Potter* and his sequel book *Rowling Revisited*, Dr. James W. Thomas points out the humor, puns, foreshadowing and literary parallels in the Potter books. In *Rowling Revisted*, readers will especially find useful three extensive appendixes – "Fantastic Beasts and the Pages Where You'll Find Them," "Quidditch Through the Pages," and "The Books in the Potter Books." Dr. Thomas makes re-reading the Potter books even more rewarding and enjoyable.

Deathly Hallows Lectures:
The Hogwarts Professor Explains Harry's Final Adventure
John Granger

In *The Deathly Hallows Lectures*, John Granger reveals the finale's brilliant details, themes, and meanings. *Harry Potter* fans will be surprised by and delighted with Granger's explanations of the three dimensions of meaning in *Deathly Hallows*. Ms. Rowling has said that alchemy sets the "parameters of magic" in the series; after reading the chapter-length explanation of *Deathly Hallows* as the final stage of the alchemical Great Work, the serious reader will understand how important literary alchemy is in understanding Rowling's artistry and accomplishment.

Hog's Head Conversations: Essays on Harry Potter
Travis Prinzi, Editor

Ten fascinating essays on Harry Potter by popular Potter writers and speakers including John Granger, James W. Thomas, Colin Manlove, and Travis Prinzi.

Sociology and Harry Potter: 22 Enchanting Essays on the Wizarding World
Jenn Simms, editor

Modeled on an Introduction to Sociology textbook. this books is not simply about the series, but also used the series to facilitate reader's understanding of the discipline of sociology and a development of a sociological approach to viewing social reality. It is a case of high quality academic scholarship written in a form and on a topic accessible to non-academics. As such, it is written to appeal to Harry Potter fans and the general reading public. Contributors include professional sociologists from eight countries.

Harry Potter, Still Recruiting:
An Inner Look at Harry Potter Fandom
Valerie Frankel, editor

The Harry Potter phenomenon has created a new world: one of Quidditch in the park, lightning earrings, endless parodies, a new genre of music, and fan conferences of epic proportions. This book attempts to document everything - exploring costuming, crafting, gaming, and more, with essays and interviews straight from the multitude of creators. From children to adults, fans are delighting the world with an explosion of captivating activities and experiences, all based on Rowling's delightful series.

Christian Living

The Living Word of the Living God:
A Beginner's Guide to Reading and Understanding the Bible
Rev. Tom Furrer

This book is based on over 20 years experience of teaching the Bible to confirmation classes at Episcopal churches in Connecticut. Chapters from Genesis to Revelation.

Keys to Growth: Meditations on the Acts of the Apostles
Will Vaus

Every living thing or person requires certain ingredients in order to grow, and if a thing or person is not growing, it is dying. *The Acts of the Apostles* is a book that is all about growth. Will Vaus has been meditating and preaching on *Acts* for the past 30 years. In this volume, he offers the reader forty-one keys from the entire book of Acts to unlock spiritual growth in everyday life.

Open Before Christmas: Devotional Thoughts For The Holiday Season
Will Vaus

Author Will Vaus seeks to deepen the reader's knowledge of Advent and Christmas leading up to Epiphany. Readers are provided with devotional thoughts for each day that help them to experience this part of the Church Year perhaps in a more spiritually enriching way than ever before.

"Seasoned with inspiring, touching, and sometimes humorous illustrations .... I found his writing immediately engaging and, the more I read, the more I liked it. God has touched my heart by reading Open Before Christmas, and I believe he will touch your heart too."
    The Rev. David Beckmann, Founder of The C.S. Lewis Society of Chattanooga

www.ingramcontent.com/pod-product-compliance
Lightning Source LLC
Chambersburg PA
CBHW060452080526
44584CB00015B/1410